THE RILKE LECTURES

Philosophy

Religion Myth Poetry

Psychology

WINDOWS INTO THE WISDOM OF THE SOPHIANIC CROSS

DANIEL JOSEPH POLIKOFF

CHIRON PUBLICATIONS • ASHEVILLE, NORTH CAROLINA

www.ChironPublications.com

Interior and cover design by Danijela Mijailovic

Printed primarily in the United States of America.

ISBN 978-1-68503-675-1 paperback
ISBN 978-1-68503-676-8 hardcover
ISBN 978-1-68503-677-5 electronic
ISBN 978-1-68503-678-2 limited edition paperback
ISBN 978-1-68503-679-9 limited edition hardcover

Library of Congress Cataloging-in-Publication Data

Names: Polikoff, Daniel Joseph, 1957- author
Title: The Rilke lectures : philosophy, religion, myth, poetry, psychology : windows into the wisdom of the Sophianic cross / Daniel Joseph Polikoff.
Description: Asheville, North Carolina : Chiron Publications, [2026] |

Includes bibliographical references. | Summary: "Originally prepared for a Pacifica Graduate Institute course on The Poetic Basis of Mind, these eight lectures stand on their own as a unique and cohesive treatment of many core concerns of the soul. As a unified whole, the lecture-essays focus upon dynamics internal to what the author (only now, years after their original composition) has come to call "the Sophianic Cross." That aegis includes not only psychology and art, but myth, religion, and philosophy as well, all pictured in relation to one another in the form of the cross-like configuration visible on this book's cover"-- Provided by publisher.
Identifiers: LCCN 2026021339 (print) | LCCN 2026021340 (ebook) | ISBN 9781685036768 hardcover | ISBN 9781685036751 paperback | ISBN 9781685036799 limited edition hardback | ISBN 9781685036782 limited edition paperback | ISBN 9781685036775 ebook

Subjects: LCSH: Rilke, Rainer Maria, 1875-1926 | Psychology and literature

Classification: LCC PT2635.I65 Z83545 2026 (print) | LCC PT2635. I65 (ebook)
LC record available at https://lccn.loc.gov/2026021339
LC ebook record available at https://lccn.loc.gov/2026021340

ALSO BY DANIEL JOSEPH POLIKOFF

CREATIVE NONFICTION/HISTORY

Rue Rilke

Reset or Renaissance Vol. 1
Two Roads: An American Scholar's Covid Chronicle

Reset or Renaissance Vol. 2
Apocalypse of the Modern Mind: Covid and the Dialectic of Enlightenment

LITERARY CRITICISM

In the Image of Orpheus: Rilke—A Soul History

POETRY

Dragon Ship

The Hands of Stars

TRANSLATION

Sonnets to Orpheus

Parzival/Gawain: Two Plays
An edited translation of ***Der Gral*** by A.M. Miller

Contents

These lectures are dedicated to

their listeners

first and foremost,
the students at Pacifica Graduate Institute

Preface

These lectures were written for the course I began teaching in the DJA program at Pacifica Graduate Institute in 2017. DJA stands (as the Pacifica website kindly reminds me) for "Depth Psychology with a specialization in Jungian and Archetypal Studies." What is a course revolving around the life and work of a poet—Rainer Maria Rilke—doing in a *psychology* program?

Anyone familiar with James Hillman's oeuvre should not have too much difficulty answering that question. Archetypal psychology (offspring of Hillman's peculiar genius) makes what Hillman calls "the poetic basis of mind" the linchpin of its attempt to place and keep *soul at the center* of psychological praxis. It is therefore only natural that, when this Rilke course was adopted into Pacifica's core curriculum two years after its inception, it was no longer one of a number of electives listed under the umbrella of "Post-Jungian Critiques and Perspectives" but was renamed "The Poetic Basis of Mind." As the First Lecture ("Depth Psychology as

Depth Aesthetics") makes clear, if one is going to take that phrase seriously and explore the novel terrain it opens, one can do no better than a concerted study of a poet who not only lived and worked during the seminal years of depth psychology (Rilke, like Jung, was born in 1875) but qualifies as one of the most consummate lyric poets of all time.

These lectures were written roughly six years after the publication of my major opus on the same Rilke-Hillman theme, *In the Image of Orpheus: Rilke—A Soul History.*[1] My Pacifica students read most of that lengthy tome for the course. In preparing these lectures, I consequently faced a distinct challenge. How might I say something about Rilke and depth psychology that I had not already said in the book?

Any concern I had on that score quickly dissolved once I set to work. This series of lectures can serve as an introduction to (or perhaps distillation of) the in-depth treatment of the convergence of archetypal psychology and poetry offered in the *Soul History*. They are, however, also much more than that. These eight lectures stand on their own as a unique and cohesive treatment of many core concerns of the soul, and pursue diverse threads not taken up in the *Soul History.* As a unified whole, the lecture-essays focus upon dynamics internal to what (only now, years after their original composition[2]) I call "the Sophianic Cross." That aegis includes not only psychology and art but myth, religion, and philosophy as well, all pictured in relation to one another in the form of the crosslike configuration visible on this book's cover.[3]

In tilling this fertile ground, the lectures attempt to disclose something of the essence of Rilke's contribution to not only poetry but the destiny of humanity. While that contribution was initially proffered in the first quarter of the 20th century, it constitutes an embassy our world desperately needs to recall and honor now, as the first quarter of the 21st comes to its own rather terrifying conclusion. I can think of no better way to indicate the aim and force of these lectures than by citing these lines from the Seventh:

> The poet Rilke read the Bible and the Quran not to absorb theology or codes of moral law but to empower him to speak with a voice of kindred power and authority, to inspire and to strengthen him in his own prophetic calling, the high mission of giving voice to the Word as it will and must be spoken, not at the foot of Sinai three millennia ago, or Jerusalem's temple steps two thousand some-odd years before his—before our—time; but far more urgently *here* and *now*, on the threshing floor of modernity,

> that *dürftiger Zeit* (needy time) when the God—or gods—that were, are no more, and the God—or gods—to come are yet to be; are yet to reveal themselves so as to shake the earth beneath our feet and thunder admonition at the senseless brutality that, more and more, masquerades as humanity on the face of the globe.

Given the time prescribed for each of the lectures (30 minutes), they are all fairly short. Consequently, this collection of the eight lectures comprises a relatively short book. Even so, I can assure my reader that these pages hold more of *original* worth than all the data centers in the world ever will. In terms of *style,* they are, above all, themselves *poetic,* and it is precisely in these darkest of times that we need all the poetry we can find, be that offered in sonnet or in lecture form. So, sit back, relax, open your soul, and (like the deer gathering around Orpheus at the foot of the tree) listen in.

First Lecture

"That is Art" - Depth Psychology as Depth Aesthetics

ENTRANCE

Whoever you are: in the evening, step out
of the room, in which you know everything;
for yours is the last house before all that is far
—whoever you are.
With your eyes, so weary they scarcely free
themselves from the worn-out threshold,
you very slowly lift one black tree
and place it against the sky: slender, alone.
And you have made the world. And it is immense
and like a word, which continues to grow
in silence. And as your will grasps its sense,
your eyes gently let it go . . .[4]

Welcome. We begin in the wake of a poem—a poem that speaks of leaving behind the already-known, the all-too-familiar; a poem that images the soul's desire to cross an invisible threshold and look out beyond the space of the the room in which it has long contained itself—rather comfortably, as if it were genuinely at home there—but nonetheless after a fashion that delimits it, that unduly confines its restless vision, vision that yearns to move towards unknown reaches of being as if mysteriously called. It is a poem of setting out, of going forth anew, and yet, of doing so without really going much of anywhere at all, for it is not our literal person that the poet invites (or commands) to venture forth, but the eye of the mind and the heart of the soul. The body need only take one small step (a little step that is, even so, a great stride) in order that our vision may be free to wander—to light, perhaps, upon the branch of some distant archetypal object so that we may *see* what can be made of it—this new world—and so of the self thus become, no resident or house-sitter, but a creator, a bearer of the living word, a *psyche-logos* or speaker of soul.

So is it that I want to begin by sketching the rationale for this particular version of this course: DJA 770, *Post-Jungian Critiques and Perspectives*. As is perhaps evident already, our approach here will be a rather uncommon one, for while psychology—the speech of the soul—will certainly remain our constant concern, our mode of exploration may be somewhat unfamiliar insofar as it takes direction from the life and work of a poet, the poet who has ushered us into this space of conversation: Rainer Maria Rilke.

Does this calling upon a poet—a gesture not so far removed from the traditional invocation of a muse—imply a kind of desertion of our prescribed field? I think not—*unless* we limit our idea of psychology to that familiar room within which it has long resided, confining its vision within the walls of restrictive disciplinary definition.

There is naturally precedent within the field itself for that fateful step across the threshold, eloquent and forceful precedent set by one of Pacifica's own guiding spirits. James Hillman has called attention to the strange contrivance of limiting the putative subject of psychology to any narrow disciplinary frame. For if soul is the heart of human being, must its living essence not predate and transcend any such restriction? Must the study of psychology then not be the study of human nature and culture as a whole? Human culture, human history, human life—but not the outward effects or external form of such, but the secret driving force, the spiritual origin and cause, the soul of all that is said and done.

And so the theoretical basis for our course will be Hillman's way (a way at once both ancient and novel) of seeing or regarding soul; what he himself calls, in his magnum opus, his "revisioning of psychology."[5]

I know you have all studied that book, and your prior work with it should stand us in good stead. Yet just in case anyone thinks he or she knows that book already, let me emphasize that it is no simple task truly to recognize just how fundamental—how radical—Hillman's *Revisioning* really is. His transformative project does indeed strike at the root of our very notion of what "psychology" is or may be, both in theory and in practice. So here, at the outset of this course, I want to highlight one cornerstone of Hillman's *Revisioning.* I want to do so in connection with the lecture that Hillman gave at Eranos in 1979, shortly after the publication of *Revisioning Psychology.*

The Thought of the Heart[6] may not be regarded as one of the weightier of Hillman's works. A long talk rather than a full-length book, it might rightly be considered less substantial than *Revisioning*, or *Myth of Analysis,*[7] or *Dreams of the Underworld.*[8] Even so, I would claim that it is a truly foundational text, for it is in this lecture that Hillman most explicitly elaborates the single premise that—more than any other—grounds his unique vision of psychology and catalyzes the paradigm shift I believe his work demands.

In *Revisioning,* Hillman places great importance upon what he calls "the poetic basis of mind," a formulation which he borrows from Jung, and one which calls prominent attention to the essentially *imaginative* character of the psyche. As his own articulation of the poetic basis of mind illustrates, Jung himself lent credence to the notion that the (linked) ideas of *imagination* and *creativity* qualify as constitutive and defining aspects of the psyche. Even so, in *The Thought of the Heart*, Hillman takes a further step (is this the step over the threshold?); a step which, on one level, may appear natural and even obvious, and yet even so is one that Jung himself manfully resisted. In *The Thought of the Heart*, Hillman declares that the psyche's essential nature lies, above all, in its intrinsic relation to beauty; asserts that any psychology worthy of the name must be grounded in *aesthetics*—the soul's capacity to experience, perceive, judge, and engender beauty.

Hillman is clear and emphatic on this score. Let me reread some of the critical passages for you. Drawing upon illustrious poets and philosophers and, in particular, the Latin author Apuleius's tale of Psyche and Eros, Hillman writes:

> The soul is born in beauty and feeds on beauty, requires beauty for its life. If we read Plato the

> way Plotinus did, and understand Psyche the way Apuleius did, and experience soul as did Petrarca and Dante, then *psyche is the life of our aesthetic responses,* that sense of taste in relation with things, that thrill or pain, disgust or expansion of breast: those primordial aesthetic reactions of the heart are soul itself speaking. Psyche's first trait, and the way we know her first, is neither by her labors, the work of soul-making, nor by her sufferings for love, nor in her oppression in lostness, the absence and deprivation of soul—these in the Apuleian tale all come later. We know her first by her primary characteristic given with her nature: Psyche is beautiful.[9]

Psyche is the life of our aesthetic responses—the phrase bears repeating. Hillman himself puts it in italics. Note, too, that when Hillman writes that "those primordial aesthetic reactions of the heart are *soul itself speaking,*" he is telling us that those reactions, however we respond or represent them, comprise the core, the heart of psychology itself, at least if we take the root of the word itself seriously.

Hillman expresses astonishment at the fact that modern psychology has, in fact, historically done just the opposite; has framed, and reframed, itself in willful neglect of this most essential truth of soul:

> How is it possible that beauty has played such a central and obvious part in the history of the soul and its thought, and yet is absent in modern psychology? Imagine—decades of depth psychology without a thought to beauty![10]

Hillman goes on to detail how psychology has marginalized aesthetic concerns, reducing fundamental features of the soul's character to undesirable derivative manifestations ("anima fascinations, immature idealizations of repression, unrelated narcissism, typically puer aestheticizing") that occlude rather than express the soul's innermost nature. Indeed, including himself in the illustrious class of those who have sinned against the goddess of beauty, Hillman offers this unequivocal expression of the primacy that should, by right, be awarded to aesthetic concerns within the province of the soul:

> In our psychological interpretations of Psyche (Neumann, von Franz, Hillman, Ulanov) we have mistaken her beauty as a mere motif to be understood, rather than as the essential

> characteristic of Psyche's image, a mistake which requires a new reading of the tale in terms of the soul's essentially aesthetic nature.
>
> If beauty is not given full place in our work with psyche, then the soul's essential realization cannot occur. And, a psychology that does not start in aesthetics—as Psyche's tale starts in beauty and as Aphrodite is the *psyché tou kosmou* or soul in all things—cannot claim to be truly psychology since it omits this essential trait of the soul's nature . . . A full depth psychology expressing the nature of Psyche must also be a depth aesthetics.[11]

It is easy enough to parrot Hillman's phrases, but what would it mean, practically and theoretically, to take his words to heart and attempt to reenvision psychology from an essentially aesthetic standpoint? What could a depth psychology that was also a "depth aesthetics" conceivably look like? How, for instance, might we read the myth of Psyche anew, taking "the soul's essentially aesthetic nature" as a point of departure?

This is no easy task. Hillman as much as admits that he himself, despite devoting an entire book to Psyche's tale (his *Myth of Analysis*), did not really manage it. But why not? Why are the psychological cards seemingly so stacked against such aesthetic enterprise?

Here we might well remember Jung, and the voice—the inner, imaginal voice of the woman, the "brilliant psychopath"—who told him that what he was doing when he was painting and writing his fantasies was making or creating *art.* (Her precise words—"That is art"—could not have been more direct.[12]) Jung, as we know, rejected the claim and silenced the voice that uttered it, declaring that if what he was doing was in fact art, it would carry neither intellectual nor moral weight; would be, that is, nothing more than ornamental to the soul's essential concerns with the True and the Good, with knowledge and virtue.

Jung could have known better because he was, after all, steeped in Kant, whose critical philosophy grounded Jung's own psychological epistemology, and who tentatively identified the *aesthetic* as the necessary mediation between *theoretical* and *practical* judgment. Similarly, Schiller, in his idealist transformation of Kant, construes the aesthetic as the indispensable mediator between the Ideal and the Real and so (in his famous *Letters*[13]) the very heart of the *education* of the human being, which is to say, the *drawing out* of its soul.

And Jung might have known better (as Hillman observes), because Plato and Plotinus, and all who follow their ancient stream, understand beauty as essentially *connate* with the Idea of the Good, and so with *both* morality *and* the seat of truth. That is a position that Jung vehemently repudiates, insisting upon a critical separation of beauty and goodness, and the consequent devaluation of the former, in the name of what he touts as "more than a thousand years of Christian differentiation."[14]

What precisely this "differentiation" is, what it really entails, is a nice question. In my mind, the "differentiation" Jung alludes to here has a great deal to do with the division at the core of human being that Hillman addresses in connection with his discussion of "the heart of Harvey." In that context, we are speaking, literally, of the division of the heart into two distinct chambers separated by an impenetrable wall. Yet, as Hillman implies, that literal, physiological splitting has wide-ranging historical overtones. For the split between right and left suggests—in the heart no less than the brain—a decisive cleavage of Mind and Heart, Thought and Feeling, Science and Religion. Harvey published his discoveries a scant decade before Descartes's *Discourse on Method*,[15] which epochal text enshrined the radical dualism of Mind and Body, Subject and Object, Spirit and Sense in the temple of the Western intellect. That fateful dualism, in turn, supplied the metaphysical foundation for the Scientific Revolution already underway and gathering a head of steam that would send it, screeching with irresistible power, down the rail of history towards the busy station of the present day.

Now this is all very relevant to our concerns. For what Jung did was to reject Art in the name of that (supposedly) rational and objective Science that has (as Richard Tarnas observes in *The Passion of the Western Mind*[16]) paradoxically become the religion or faith of the modern world, the chief arbiter of Truth and ultimate Reality. The scientific paradigm—that intellectual descendant of Harvey and Descartes—founded, grounded, and still informs the praxis and disciplinary definition of modern psychology. Psychology emerged as a branch of *Naturwissenschaft* (natural science) and tacitly adopted the mode of knowing, the standards of truth and meaning, associated therewith; an epistemology inextricably linked to a rationalist and even mechanistic interpretation of the core of nature and of the human being (again, the heart of Harvey). And isn't the language of psychology—even modern depth psychology—still generally stamped by the norms of knowledge derivative of the "objective" epistemology of science? Don't those norms still largely dictate the genres and modes of linguistic expression we generally recognize as representative of real and valid (and so morally binding) knowledge, the sort of discourse we credit as demonstrative of intellectual mastery of the subject at hand? Just look at the rhetorical mode of any dissertation abstract, and I think you are likely to see (or rather *hear*) what I mean.

And yet—let us stop for a moment; halt and get off the train to gain time for relevant reflection. Is not the subject of psychology, the source of our interest and concern, the psyche itself; or, rather (as Hillman may persuade us to say) Psyche—with a capital "P"—herself? And can this subject—can Psyche—be truly "known" after the fashion or idiom of a concept-dominated scientific language that inherently strives to distance, objectify, measure, master, and so—ultimately—command and control?

I am perhaps exaggerating a little to make my point, yet only a little. Why did Carl Jung feel compelled to silence the feminine voice that declared his work "art"? Why did he dismiss the mythopoetic masterpiece of his contemporary, James Joyce (whose early *Portrait of the Artist as a Young Man*[17] contains a pivotal discussion of Thomist aesthetics that catalyzes Stephen Daedalus's conversion to a religion of beauty) as immoral self-indulgence? Why did he hide his *Red Book*[18]—which, by his own admission, supplied the *prima materia* of his psychology—and hand down to us, as the *representative body* of his work, a corpus of many far less poetic texts that, while borrowing imagery from others (patient's dreams, alchemical texts, artworks) themselves traffic largely in analytic concepts? Why does he give us (figuratively speaking) the Baptist's head on a plate and not Salomé dancing? Can we even begin to understand one without the other?

In fact, for all the inestimable value of his analytic psychology, Jung did not give us anything like an adequate account of Psyche *"as the life of our aesthetic responses."* His version of Psyche, his vision of her character, did not tend in that direction; on the contrary.

But Hillman imagines otherwise. In his *Thought of the Heart*, Hillman (who began his intellectual career writing short stories in—where else?—Dublin) embraces Aphrodite and reminds us that in her ancient, polytheistic universe (one that predates all those years of "Christian differentiation" and Jung's own fin de siècle sense of beauty as mere aestheticism), the aesthetic and the moral, the Beautiful and the Good, cannot well be sundered; *that indeed the first functions as the visible, the perceptible, legible path towards the second.*

But how then do we recognize her (Aphrodite's) touch; how do we see her at play, or work? Referring once more to that ancient world view, Hillman writes:

> For beauty there, then . . . means *the form of what is presented*, that which is breathed in,

> *aisthesis,* and by which the value of each particular thing strikes the heart, the organ of aesthetic perception, where judgments are heartfelt responses, not merely critical mental reflections. . . . For the thought of the heart, reflection is not bending backward (*CW* 8: para. 241), a movement afterward in time, away from the object in space as it is transformed by psychic images and judged in the mind. Rather, reflection refers to the very aesthetic quality of any event, its sheen and shape, the luster of its skin. Event itself as image.

Where, then, may we best look for tangible exhibition of such an angle of vision?

Imagine Rilke, living in Paris in 1902, commissioned to write a monograph on the great sculptor Auguste Rodin and so assiduously studying the old master and his methods. These inevitably involve close observation. On assignment, so to speak, from Rodin, Rilke goes to the *Jardin des Plantes*, the Botanical Garden, and encounters (among myriad other things) a black panther in a cage. He observes it carefully, and—later—writes:

THE PANTHER

The passing of the bars fatigues his gaze
so much, that it can hold no more.
To him it is as if each bar were a maze
that led to another and another barred door.

The quiet pacing of the strong and supple limbs
that turn around the very smallest sphere
is like a dance of power around the rims
of circles, that hold a great will numb in there.

Only seldom does the pupil's curtain slide
soundlessly up—. Then an image enters,
ripples through the tensely stilled stride
and ceases where the rhythm centers.[19]

"The aesthetic quality of an event, its sheen and shape, the luster of its skin. Event itself as image." Does not Rilke's poem *enact* what Hillman is talking about with a precision that is, in this instance, almost uncannily literal? If so, can we fairly say that this poem is, in and of itself . . . *psychology?* It is indubitably a record of aesthetic response. That is, evidently, what a poem (or any artwork) is. Correlatively, a poet's oeuvre, the body of his work, presents—in fulfillment of Hillman's

prescription—soul *in the representative form of "the life of our aesthetic responses."*

And so it is to some degree self-evident that if we are to understand psychology as Hillman reenvisions it, we may—perhaps *must*—begin with the poets, the artists; with the work of those whose vocation is and (long before the advent of what we now call "psychology") always has been to give us (direct from the source, unvarnished by over much critical mental reflection) the speech of the soul.

Poetic speech can and does give voice to soul in part because—under the auspices of Aphrodite and the Thought of the Heart—it does not acknowledge the divided heart, the heart of Harvey and of Descartes, that splits apart Mind and Body, Spirit and Sense. Look at the integral picture of the panther painted by Rilke's words. Can we begin to separate Concept and Percept, Thought and Image as we experience the poem and the thing to which it lends expression? I think not. In this, it is emblematic of the nature of art itself, which derives from that original soul, that virgin psyche, which (precisely because it is essentially and originally the creative mediation between the intelligible and sensible dimensions of being) does *not* present these poles as separate, as divided by an impenetrable wall.

That is as much to say—flat out—that poetry (and by this we mean not only poems but also the poetic element in all forms of expression) is the first and primary speech of the soul, the original *logos* of the *psyche*. The critical, analytical discourse of psychology is inherently dependent upon this first, essentially symbolic language, which consequently supplies theoretical reflection with its primary source material.

Let us elaborate. Discussing the psyche's essential nature—beauty—in the context of the myth of Psyche and Eros, Hillman, setting his own work aside, declares the need for "a new reading of the tale in terms of the soul's essentially aesthetic nature." How might we translate or interpret that proposal? If a human soul were to live after a fashion singularly dedicated to beauty, devoting his life to the creation of works that give fit expression to most every step of the long and winding way on the path towards realizing lasting communion with Beauty and with Love, would not his or her life-work be worthy of attention, and might not interpretation of the interwoven fabric of that life and that work qualify as the "new reading of the tale" Hillman envisions?

It is my conviction (and, judging by his popularity, not only mine) that Rainer Maria Rilke is an exemplary instance of such a soul. Consequently, the book that will function as the primary text for this course (*In the Image of Orpheus: Rilke—A Soul History*[20]) may be understood as my attempt to fulfill Hillman's vision of "a new reading of the tale" of Psyche and Eros. Coincidentally, it may also be understood as an effort to begin to model a depth psychology that is, simultaneously and inseparably, a depth aesthetics.

Next week, we will begin that soul journey in earnest.

I must close now, without having directly addressed *Rue Rilke.*[21] Even so, most everything I have said here is highly relevant to that text—and vice versa. As its front matter states, *Rue Rilke* offers a kind of personal introduction to my connection to the poet who will (along with Hillman) serve as a guide for the journey we are embarking upon. It is not always an easy text, but I would encourage those of you who have time, energy, and interest to read more in it than I was able to assign, as the shape and transformative force of the pilgrimage only really reveals itself gradually. In any event, the material will help provide—along with Hillman's *The Thought of the Heart*—a fit point of departure.

Bon Voyage.

Second Lecture

"Bittersweet Eros" – At the Lyric Fount

In the first lecture, I alluded to the truth that aesthetic or poetic expression gives voice to the soul and bridges the difference between mind and matter, the two "halves" of the cosmos effectively sundered in the heart of Harvey, Cartesian dualism, and the Scientific Revolution. Today I want to discuss further relations of spirit, soul, and body in order to underscore the intimate, indeed original and indissoluble, connection between the soul and poetic speech, granting special attention to the paradigmatic genre of the latter: namely, the lyric.

Spirit, soul, body: These terms are not exactly self-explanatory. How could they be when the *Weltanschauung* (worldview) that underlies the modern era premises itself upon an effective elision of the middle term, soul? In fact, in his landmark essay *Peaks and Vales*, Hillman makes emphatically clear that while the likes of Harvey and Descartes solidified the dualistic cast of the Western mind, the mold had already been authoritatively shaped by the Church as early as 869. Hillman:

> At that Council at Constantinople the soul lost its dominion. Our anthropology, our idea of human nature, devolved from a tripartite cosmos of spirit, soul, and body (or matter), to a dualism of spirit (or mind) and body (or matter) . . . . We are in this room this evening because we are moderns in search of a soul, as Jung once put it. We are still in search of reconstituting that third place, that intermediate realm of psyche—from which we were exiled by theological, spiritual men more than a thousand years ago: long before Descartes and the dichotomies attributed to him, long before the Enlightenment and modern positivism and scientism. These ancient historical events are responsible for the malnourished root of our psychological culture and of the culture of each of our souls.[22]

Hillman consistently understands a reclamation of soul, and the consequent restoration of a tripartite rather than dualistic cosmology, as central to the project of archetypal psychology, a psychology that "puts soul at the center." Yet what does this really mean, and (more critically) how is such a project not only announced but accomplished?

Both the Introduction and Appendix I of *In the Image of Orpheus* expend some effort sketching a basic understanding of the trinity of terms spirit, soul, and body. As discussed in the Appendix, the last stanza of Charles Wright's poem "Indian Summer II" provides a particularly stark statement of the diametrically opposed characters of the realms of spirit, on the one hand, and matter (or body) on the other:

> We live in two landscapes, as Augustine might
> have said,
> One that is eternal and divine,
> and one that's just the back yard,
> Dead leaves and dead grass in November,
> purple in spring.[23]

As the poem implies, the world of temporal existence is a domain of change, indelibly marked by the *transience* of things subject to death and decay. This is no mere poetic fancy. Even in our own materialistic age, a little deliberate reflection may bring home the time-honored truth that the so-called "real" world is irreducibly ephemeral. Nothing in it lasts or *is* what it *is* permanently, but is rather always in the process of disappearing or becoming something else. So it is that the human soul, if not thoroughly anaestheticized (as is of course a prevalent danger in our frenetic society) inevitably seeks connection with more permanent verities, yearns for engagement with a sphere of being that is not mere appearance, longs for some relation to an eternal or divine order which can lend a sense of pattern, meaning, and purpose to mortal existence. That desire, that primal yearning, qualifies as a defining characteristic of the soul itself, the vital nature of which consists in constant translation, or movement between, the spiritual and material poles of existence.

It is the function of primary symbolic expressions of the soul (myth, ritual, religion) to perform just such acts of translation and so satisfy the embodied self's longing for spiritual sustenance. When inherited forms of culture no longer perform that function, when the rehearsal of sanctioned myths and the observance of established rites fail to confer any living sense of participation in a more permanent order, the soul loses coherent sense of its own identity and undergoes spiritual crisis. Innumerable authors have identified such a state of disoriented alienation as the ground-tone of modernity.

James Hollis, by way of C.G. Jung, associates the emergence of the field of psychology itself with just such a state of crisis. Hollis writes:

> The core condition of our time has been manifest as a collective spiritual wound, one perhaps as traumatic as an amputation. Jung noted that psychology was the last of the so-called social sciences to be invented because the insights which it seeks were previously in the domain of tribal mythologies and institutionalized religions. When moderns fell off the roof of the medieval cathedral, Jung wrote, they fell into the abyss of the Self. Affective linkage to the cosmos, nature, and the community was once available via tribal creation stories, heroic legends, and transformative rituals. Wth the loss of those connective rites and mythic images, the problem of identity and the task of cosmic location, or spiritual grounding, becomes an individual dilemma.[24]

Rainer Maria Rilke was born in 1875, the same year as Carl Jung. Rilke's life, like Jung's, thus spanned the formative years of what we today call depth psychology. Reading the initial pages of Rilke's soul history (including the religiously charged circumstances of his birth and his fraught adolescent development), we recognize that the dilemma Hollis describes was very much the young Rilke's own, and indeed all the more powerfully so for his growing up (again like Jung) in a devoutly Christian household. For those with such a background often come to feel with special force the insufficiency of their spiritual inheritance. Concomitantly, they may experience, too, how the burden of spiritual self-definition falls, with tremendous weight, squarely upon their own *individual* shoulders.

I want here to take a step back for a moment to gain historical perspective on this modern predicament. I want, that is, to review certain dynamic changes in the underlying relations of what we are calling spirit, soul, and body as such have transpired over the course of centuries. By so doing, I hope to prepare the ground for a deeper understanding of what Rilke was up against and what (consciously or unconsciously) he may have hoped to achieve by taking upon himself the calling of the poet at the turn of the 20th century.

James Hollis alludes to older forms of culture spiritually nourished and sustained by "tribal creation stories, heroic legends, and transformative rituals."

Viewed from an intellectual historical perspective, or in the light of the evolution of human consciousness, such premodern cultures effectively *predate* any decisive splitting of spirit and matter. This means that in such cultures, what we are calling spirit, soul, and body co-exist in a more or less unified, largely undifferentiated state; indeed, a state wherein the space of individual soul-consciousness *which is opened by a certain critical separation of spirit and matter* does not exist as such—at least, not in anything like its modern form.

This insight may serve to call attention to a provocative truth. A Hillmanian critique of the dualistic splitting of spirit and matter (and consequent elision of soul) may be very much in order at this point in time. Even so, it is important to recognize that—at another, earlier phase of development—a novel separation of spirit and matter must have functioned as a precondition for the original emergence of "soul" per se, by which I mean a mode of individual consciousness possessing relative autonomy vis-a-vis the universality of spirit, on the one hand, and the particularity and manifest contingency of body, on the other.

Now (to pursue this line of thought still further) neither Descartes nor Harvey nor even the first millennium Church Councils represent the earliest phase of the critical separation of spirit and matter I am evoking here.

Within a Greek context, such could perhaps be traced to the ascension of the Olympian Gods (which would include their triumph over the earthbound Titans), which event established divinity in a transcendent, celestial sphere at significant remove from all earthly doings (even if, of course, the Olympian Gods remained very concerned and indeed involved with mortal matters). Later, with the advent of philosophy, this difference translated into the Platonic division of the intelligible and sensible worlds.[25] Correlatively, within the quite different religious culture of the Levant, we could point to the Jewish idea of a transcendent God who ultimately, in his Christianized version, becomes "Our Father in Heaven," a deity that (like the Olympian Gods) remains concerned with the Earth, but does not abide or have his home there—certainly not in the way the spirits of primal religions abide in animals, trees, and all kinds of sacred earthly places. In the Judeo-Christian tradition, the Earth and indeed the creation as a whole is in fact fabricated out of nothing *(ex nihilo)* and is not consubstantial with God.

The seed of the radical dualism we see in Harvey and Descartes is already planted in these earlier discriminations between Spirit and Matter, Transcendent Divinity and Mundane World, Heaven and Earth, Eternal and Temporal or Intelligible and Sensible realms. Now, to reiterate: While the modern *polarized* form of this separation may well be associated with the spiritual dislocation characteristic of modernity, we can only speak of an elision of the soul if, at some point, the soul effectively came into its own as a third intermediary term. According to the classicist Bruno Snell, that epochal development took place roughly between the seventh and middle of the fifth century B.C.E., a period coincident with the emergence of Greek lyric poetry. Nor was such coincidence accidental; on the contrary. According to Snell, *it was precisely in and through the development of lyric expression that the mode of individual consciousness we today call "soul" or "psyche" first came into existence.*

This truth—if accepted as such—implies a highly significant corollary, namely: anything and everything we may think of under the aegis of "psychology" ultimately derives from (and, in its theoretical or analytical guise, takes form as a kind of reflection upon) that mode of consciousness originally engendered by lyric speech.

As moderns, we are liable to forget this. Hillman, as well as authors like Hollis and (yet more explicitly) Robert Romanyshyn,[26] tries to remind us of it. And Rilke . . . Rilke knew it so deeply that (deliberately eschewing psychoanalysis, as he did shortly before penning his prophetic *Elegies*) he instinctively devoted himself, heart and soul, to it, so that his life and work unfold as a revelation of this primary, this original truth of the soul; a revelation we cannot afford *not* to read closely, again and again.

Very well, but how is it that Greek lyric poets like Archilochus and (above all) the immortal Sappho performed the miracle and birthed the soul? Let us, with Snell as guide, review some of the signal features of this development, for doing so will put us in a position better to appreciate how Rilke, one of the purest lyric poets of all time, renewed that originative act while standing at the threshold of modernity two-and-a-half millennia later.

To understand something of the emergence of the lyric in Greece, it is necessary first to form some conception of the mythopoetic world out of which it emerged, the world magnificently bodied forth in the Homeric epic. The Olympian Gods are alive and well here; even so, the *separation* between spiritual and material realms remains incipient. In Homer, Snell declares, "the concept of the spiritual is not divorced from the corporeal."[27] What transpires on the physical and indeed the emotional plane does so primarily (and more or less immediately) on account of divine agency. This is so because the *middle* term—which Snell identifies as individual soul or mind—has as yet not emerged into consciousness. Nor is there even a word for it:

> Homer has no one word to characterize the mind or the soul. *Psyche,* the word for soul in later Greek, has no original connection with the thinking and feeling soul. For Homer, *psyche* is the force which keeps the human being alive.[28]

Snell elaborates further:

> If we venture to say that Homer's men had as yet no knowledge of the intellect, or of the soul . . . we do not thereby mean that his characters were not capable of joy or reflection, and so forth. We merely want to stress that they did not conceive of these matters as actions of the intellect or soul; and it is in this sense that they did not know the two. As a further consequence it appears that in the early period, the 'character' of an individual is not yet recognized. Here again there is no denying that the great heroes of the Homeric poems are drawn in firm outline; and yet the reactions of an Achilles, however grand and significant, are not explicitly presented in

> their volitional or intellectual form as character, i.e. as individual intellect and individual soul.[29]

Finally, in a passage with great resonance for our theme, Snell writes:

> The first writer to feature the new concept of the soul is Heraclitus. He calls the soul of living man *psyche*; in his view man consists of body and soul, and the soul is endowed with qualities which differ radically from those of the body and the physical organs. We can safely say that these new qualities are irreconcilable with the categories of Homer's thought; he does not even dispose of the linguistic prerequisites to describe what Heraclitus predicates of the soul. The new expressions were fashioned in the period which separates Heraclitus from Homer, that is to say the era of the lyric.[30]

In *Revisioning Psychology*, Hillman identifies Heraclitus as the thinker who first articulated the metaphor that founds what we call depth psychology. Snell, for his part, continues to cite the crucial sentence from Heraclitus *and* to explain (as Hillman does not) that the pre-Socratic thinker merely rearticulated what was, essentially and originally, a poetic initiative:

> Heraclitus says: 'You could not find the ends of the soul though you travelled every way, so deep is its logos.' This notion of the depth or profundity of the soul is not unfamiliar to us; but it involves a dimension which is foreign to a physical organ or its function. To say: someone has a deep hand, or a deep ear, is nonsensical . . . In Heraclitus the image of depth is designed to throw light on the outstanding trait of the soul and its realm: that it has its own dimension, that it is not extended in space. To describe this non-spatial substance we are of course obliged to fall back on a metaphor taken from space relations. But in the last analysis Heraclitus means to assert that the soul, as contrasted with things physical, reaches into infinity. Not Heraclitus but the lyric poets who preceded him were the first to voice this new idea, that intellectual and spiritual matters have 'depth.'[31]

How, then, did the lyric poets originate the idea of a soul, a psyche characterized by depth? Another revealing passage from Snell—one that begins by quoting a line from Sappho's predecessor, Anacreon—elaborates the central issue:

> *Again I love and love not; I rave, nor do I rave.*

> The unhappy lover describes his state of struggling helplessness by the paradox that he affirms and negates one and the same thing . . . For this condition Sappho had found an equally paradoxical but even terser formulation when she wrote of the "bitter-sweet Eros." At the time her epithet was no commonplace; the coin which has now become worn with the handling of 2,500 years then bore a clear and fresh design. The epic does not yet feature such emotional discord or tension, because conditions of that sort do not exist in the area of physical operations, in whose image Homer portrays the mental processes. Sappho, with her bold neologism 'bitter-sweet', discovers the area of the soul and defines it as fundamentally distinct from the body.[32]

Thus—as might be expected from the metaphysical underpinning of the spirit, soul, body triad—*soul or psyche originally emerges as a term capable of holding tension, the conflict of opposites, within itself.*

The core of the lyric, moreover, while irreducibly centered in the affective intellect (what Hillman might call "the thought of the heart") possesses metaphysical as well as psychological depth. The lyric not only contains *emotional opposites* within its constitutive form but additionally spans the invisible space between the realms of the divine and the mortal, the universal and the particular, eternal verity and the ever-changing present.

A pair of passages from Snell illustrates this truth. Snell first tells us how lyric aims to connect the here and now *(hic et nunc)* to a more enduring order of things:

> The majority of the early Greek lyrics which have come down to us are poems composed for various festivals in honour of gods or men; their purpose is to make the present significant over and above the *hic et nunc*, to lend an air of permanence to the joy of the moment . . .[33]

Shortly thereafter, when speaking of the choral lyric that exercised such enduring influence on Western literature (and here Snell explicitly mentions Rilke, along with Goethe and Hölderlin, as poets who drew from this source), Snell emphasizes the opposite pole of the eternal/temporal equation:

> One basic difference which distinguishes the lyric from the epic is to be found in the value which the former attaches to the present. The great deeds of the past are no longer celebrated for their own sake, but because they serve to exalt the present; for the Greeks of the archaic period took an unbounded delight in the present, in everything that is alive and colourful. The tension between value and fact, between myth and actuality . . . tends to become more and more evident in the course of the two hundred years during which lyric poetry prevailed; but the present, albeit raised to the level of timelessness, remains, throughout, its immediate frame of reference.[34]

The emphasis on the present—the "here and now"—is associated with the most obvious and tangible difference between the lyric and the epic. While grand sagas are inevitably lengthy, the paradigmatic lyric—like this from Sappho—is a flicker of the candle of the heart:

> I was so happy
> believe me, I
> prayed that that
>
> night might be
> doubled for us[35]

This, of course, is a love lyric, the kind for which Sappho is most famous. And the mention of Love allows us to call attention to another, crucial way in which the lyric originally spans and holds the tension between opposites; in this connection, the poles of mortal and divine life, personal and transpersonal existence. For even while the love lyric famously initiates discourse palpably and poignantly issuing from an intimately personal center, it remains profoundly connected with and indebted to the suprapersonal, divine sources of the relevant feelings: to Eros and Aphrodite, who are directly invoked in any number of Sapphic songs. Yet even when not mentioned by name, the god and goddess are present in the very air which the newfound soul of the lyric poet breathes. Snell:

> For the death-likeness of love is, particularly in Sappho's view, the greatest tension of which the soul is capable. The early poets conceive of this

> new mode of feeling as something supernatural; a divine impulse powerful enough to determine their values for them.[36]

So it is that the new realm of personal thought and feeling—the new domain of soul— opened by the lyric poets did not involve any decisive *divorce* from the divine and universal realm of spirit mythically represented by the gods. Rather than division, it is a matter of distinction which actually initiates the possibility of genuine *relation.* The same could be said of the relation between the newfound soul and sensuously experienced world of the body. As Snell shows, in the world of the lyric poets, the soul or mind discovers itself as it distinguishes itself from the physical world. Even so, this by no means entails an estrangement from sense experience; on the contrary, it opens the path for a far more conscious and differentiated relation to such.

Although it is not possible here to elaborate all the nuanced complexities entailed in the lyric poets' discovery of soul, one more citation from Snell will serve to highlight how this discovery—which is coincidently, the discovery of *individual* consciousness (and here by "individual" I mean not merely the personal self, but an identity inherently personal and transpersonal, particular and universal at once) opens the possibility of a world characterized by a *differentiated and balanced relationship* between spirit, soul, and body. Snell:

> The law of eternal change is also a discovery of the lyric writers; it is not of the same order as the discovery of individual feeling, but it acts as its complement. The new individuality is paralleled by a new universality; the new capacity of the senses is braced by a new rational understanding. They are intimately and necessarily connected; the eternal ebb and flow is emotionally experienced, and the result is knowledge.[37]

How does all this relate to the young Rilke, to his early lyrics and to his eleven *Visions of Christ?*[38]

Rilke and the Greek lyricists are equally poets of soul, but come to the calling from dramatically different circumstances. As we have seen, the Greek lyric poets write against a background of a close, dyadic relationship between the spiritual and corporeal and the poet's originative act involves opening and inhabiting the psychic space in-between. The modern poet faces the opposite problem. Spirit and matter, heaven and earth, divine and human being had been decisively divided and pulled apart, leaving nothing in the middle but what Jung called "the abyss of Self." Rilke's voice sounds from the depth of that gulf, striving to rebuild the broken bridge of soul.

We spoke earlier about the special spiritual challenges confronting a Rilke—or a Jung—at the turn of the last century. Rilke did not write against the fertile imaginative background of the Homeric epic. Instead, the world into which he was born was doctrinally rigidified, symbolically impoverished and religiously split at the seams. In order to re-open a viable relation to the realm of spirit, Rilke—as I discuss in *In the Image of Orpheus*—had to deconstruct the dualistic presuppositions underlying his inherited world-view. His *Visions of Christ* perform this critical act by means of—not theoretical discourse—but the mythopoetic imagination.

And from what standpoint did Rilke write the *Visions?* In order to move a mountain, one need avail oneself of the infinite leverage gained from standing at the center of the universe. As his early poems show, Rilke's innate lyric genius coincided with an intimate relation to the very archetype of soul, the yearning and the inner tension and the devotion to love and the in-between state of dream—all of which devolve from the original, intermediary nature of *soul per se*, the individual consciousness perpetually suspended between the spiritual and material poles of the universe. His lyrics—even his early, relative immature ones from *Offering to the Lares* or *Dream-Crowned*[39]—overflow with the substance of soul; with emotion that is not merely the "personal feeling" of the heart of Augustine, but poetic—aesthetically *formed*—feeling that expresses itself in moving tones and affecting imagery and is powerful enough to connect the physical body of a city (Prague's church turrets "thinning to a point like pears") with the "violent ink of sky" darkening the heavens,[40] and deep enough that—if ever one were to imagine the emptying of the receptacle of the soul—"the flood would put out all the stars."[41]

So it is that Rilke—laying claim to the mantle of the lyric poets whose language invented soul in the first place—set out to re-discover and re-claim it; to re-envision the fragmented and deadened landscape of modernity as a place where spirit, soul, and body might once again be housed, cherished and held together in the kind of delicate balance that has been, from the beginning, the birthmark of beauty in the western world.

Third Lecture

"You, Neighbor God" - Rilkean Religion

The hour bows down and touches me
with its clear metallic ring:
my senses shiver. I feel I can
grasp the day as a malleable thing.

Nothing was whole before I beheld it;
all becoming stands still.
My glances are ripe, and like a bride,
to each comes the thing that it wills.

Nothing is too small for me to love
and paint great on a background of gold.
I hold it high, and know not whose
soul it will break from the mold.[42]

So begins the *Book of Monastic Life*, the first of the three books comprising Rilke's *Book of Hours* and the one most immediately inspired by his first journey to Russia with Lou Andreas-Salomé. Rilke assumes the persona of an icon-painting monk, an individual whose vocation is inseparably religious and artistic. That crucial coincidence signals the means by which the poet aims to address (and here I quote Hollis) "the task of cosmic location or spiritual grounding," the "problem of identity" that in the modern era becomes—pointedly and urgently— "an individual dilemma."[43]

We have spoken repeatedly of the spirit-matter dualism underpinning that crisis, and revisiting it again in yet another guise can help us gain a clearer picture of what Rilke is up to—and up against—in writing this book of poems originally called (simply) *"Prayers."*

In Rilke's time, religion (the dominant, Christian religion) represented one pole—the spiritual one—of the cleft heart of humanity. Science—the new, upstart faith of the modern era and one dramatically bolstered by Darwin's recent discoveries—stood, as it still stands today, for the other.

Historically speaking, Science and the Church have not always been diametrically opposed. Before the Protestant Reformation, the Church generally supported scientific investigation,[44] believing intellectual exploration of the design of the natural world quite commensurate with Christian faith. Luther and Galileo, however, changed all that. The radical German priest, preoccupied with the human being's personal relationship to God, showed little interest in the Book of Nature and insisted upon scriptural revelation as the sole source of religious truth. Galileo championed Copernicus's heliocentric theory, which many influential persons regarded as incompatible with both the letter and spirit of the Bible. Ultimately, the Church's rejection of that theory, and its persecution of Galileo, spelled the end of the era of material partnership between science and religion.[45]

That historical schism had far-reaching consequences, absolutizing the *metaphysical* split between the prevailing concepts of the spiritual and material realms of existence, driving these contrary poles so far apart that—in each case—the disfavored pole effectively fell off the map of reality altogether. Thus did Descartes's philosophic dualism transform into two contrary forms of monism.

On the one hand, science, construing matter and its laws as the beginning and end of all, emphatically denies the very existence of spirit. The title of British biologist Richard Dawkin's popular book *The God Delusion*[46] illustrates well the manner in which partisans of this view often regard the spirit of religion.

The argument on the other side tends to be a bit less unequivocal, for it is easier to deny the existence of God or Soul than it is to impugn the reality of the all-too palpable world of the senses. Even so (as discussed at some length in the fourth chapter of *In the Image to Orpheus*), Christian metaphysics and morality, taking their cue from Augustine, tends in just this direction. The transcendent almighty God figures as the source and end of all *authentic* Being. The material world, originally created *not* of divine substance but rather (in accordance with the doctrine of *creation ex nihilo*) out of nothing, remains essentially and ineradicably foreign to the divine nature. Fallen away from grace of God and indelibly marked by death, decay, and impermanence, this world appears as essentially illusory when regarded from the standpoint of Augustinian theology.

And what of the human soul? Where does it find itself in this scheme? As we discovered in reading Charles Wright's own Augustine-quoting poem, smack in the middle of nowhere; fallen into the vast chasm between the contrary poles of existence.

We have seen that Rilke himself provided an imaginative précis of that predicament in his *Visions of Christ* and strove, too, to undo the religious mythology he held responsible for it. *The Book of Hours* builds on that critical initiative but additionally takes a great creative leap forward. In this remarkable work, the poet does not concentrate so much upon *repudiating* outworn aspects of his inherited faith as upon refreshing the authentic spirit of religion, an end he aims to achieve by reclaiming the creative power hidden in the depths of the gulf between the poles, that yawning chasm Carl Jung called "the abyss of Self."

Our poet did have ample help in that project. As discussed in the *Soul History*,[47] *The Book of Hours* builds not only upon Rilke's Russia experience but upon his prior journey to Italy as well. His encounter with the genius of Renaissance art (especially Michelangelo's titanic spirit) granted Rilke an entirely new degree of consciousness of what were for him two closely intertwined facets of his own being: a heightened awareness of the mystery of the Self as such; and a new reverence for the high—indeed sacred—calling of the creative artist. The seed of the idea of donning the persona of an artist-monk in order to communicate his deepest insights into the riddle of existence were thus sown in Italian soil.

While Italy was crucial to the gestation of *The Book of Hours*, it nourished only one side of Rilke's religious sensibility, the side Lou Andreas-Salomé, in her brilliant definition of what she calls "the religious affect," describes as "the fullest and most satisfying living out of all the faculties of selfhood."[48] Rilke found inspiration flowing from the other side of Lou's equation—"the sincerest humility before an ideal experienced as divine"[49]—in Russia.

What is perhaps most striking about the project Rilke essays in *The Book of Hours* is that, unlike Nietzsche, Rilke does not strive for spiritual renewal by unequivocally repudiating religion but rather does so by way of a radical revision of the idea and image of God transmitted by Judeo-Christian tradition. Such revision was and is vitally necessary if that "third" term—the soul—is truly to reclaim its own, to rediscover the name and place originally vouchsafed to it (as we saw in the last lecture) by the Greek lyric poets.

If Renaissance and (still later) Romantic artists did, in their own more modern ways, reaffirm and rearticulate the centrality of the human soul in the larger scheme of things, they did not manage decisively to transform the theology and cosmology that continues to dominate mainstream culture. If the materialism of modern science steadfastly refuses to recognize the essentially spiritual character of the psyche, the *theological* premises of Rilke's inherited religion are not, if truth be told, much more hospitable to the individual soul seeking to compass and affirm its own unique and distinct identity. Hillman, for his part, never tires of reminding us that the popularly received forms of the Christian religion are intrinsically unpsychological, inherently antisoul.[50]

How and why is this so?

In exoteric forms of the Christian religion, the realm of spirit is dominated by (the idea or image of the) one supreme God. His angels and even his beloved Son are modulations of that sovereign power. As discussed in Chapter Four of *In the Image of Orpheus,* the Augustine-inflected concept of an almighty God leaves the individual soul precious little spiritual air to breathe. Absolute in Power, Knowledge, and Goodness; eternally perfect and self-sufficient, the Supreme Being does and cannot truly need anything from the mortal human being who dwells—not with Him in his heavenly abode—but in the ephemeral natural world that is, by virtue of man's original sin, fallen away from his Grace. In this scenario, the quintessence of the religious life, the essence of the psyche's spiritual life, consists not of the fullest exfoliation of the faculties of selfhood, but of chaste aversion to the temptations of the temporal world so that the corrupt soul may be saved. That means *reabsorbed*—without residue—into the realm of God the Father, an event mythically figured as dying and going to heaven.

This sketch of Christian religion is crude and oversimplistic. Even so, it represents in broad brushstroke the outline of the Augustinian theology that has shaped prevailing doctrines of the church. But the profound imbalance inherent in the paradigm: the disparagement of the earthly world, and the consequent depreciation of the value of the mortal soul's own being and doing (and so, we could say, its nigh exclusive emphasis on only *one* side of Lou's equation of the religious affect) could not but take its toll. For the young Rilke and countless others, the idea of spirit encoded in this theology, the God-image embedded in it, lost effective force and credibility. Lacking any satisfying account of the relatively autonomous significance of the individual human being or the enduring beauty embodied in the natural universe, it ceased to engage or move the psyche; to stir aspiration, yearning, enthusiasm, reverence, and love in the human soul.

Renaissance artists, Nietzsche (who of course famously declared the death of God), Emerson: All these influences emboldened the young poet to affirm the central value of the individual soul's own creative prerogatives[51] despite religious doctrine not inherently conducive to such. Even so, it was Lou Andreas-Salome's writings on aesthetics and (still more critically) the psychology of religion, that gave Rilke a means of understanding how he might—not reject divine agency altogether—but enter into creative dialogue with it in such a way as to liberate the individual soul's own original religious imagination and, simultaneously, revive, not the dead letter, but the *spirit* of God.

Well before Carl Jung began his professional career, Lou Salomé understood that any system of spirit (even, or especially one, such as the Judeo-Christian tradition, that embraced the idea of a transcendent godhead) inevitably rests upon a psychological footing. That is to say, she understood that the effective, living force of such a godhead is radically dependent upon the individual's soul's own idea or imagination of it. Practically speaking, this may be understood to imply (and Lou did so construe the matter) that it is the human imagination—the creative power of the soul—that originally engenders gods as such exist in the only way that can really matter to us: namely, as vital agencies in human life and consciousness. "God" cannot subsist in human culture as wholly and unreservedly Other; a perfectly transcendent force entirely alien to mortal human or *psychological* consciousness, *because even the idea and image of such a perfectly transcendent God itself take shape as a notion and image in the soul.* Such is the first premise of the psychology of religion, which phrase should be heard not to demarcate a special department of psychology that studies some other, discrete domain but rather as an articulation of the truth that what Andreas-Salomé calls the *religious affect,* the motive force of the spiritual life of the human being, *cannot* be artificially divorced from its root cause and source, namely: the imaginative life of the soul.

It is true that major strands of religious thought, including aspects of Judeo-Christian and Vedantic belief, expend tremendous psychic energy attempting to hold the thought that *any* thought or image *cannot be* the transcendent godhead itself, so that religious life unfolds along the path of a *via negativa.* And yet, while the transcendent character of the spirit (awareness that the godhead itself ultimately transcends any particular imagination the soul may form of it) remains a defining characteristic of the very idea of spirit as such may distinguished from the soul, if such a perspective is construed in such a way as *to deny the creative image-making capacity of the soul's participation in spirit*—then the authenticity of the soul itself is undercut and indeed elided, and the human psyche quickly finds itself in the abysmal predicament we have so insistently described.

Lou Andreas-Salomé's psychology of religion helped Rilke climb out of that deep religious hole. For Andreas-Salomé did not merely teach that any God-image was, in its very nature as such, originally a product of the human psyche. Such a critical and deconstructive move had already been made, and far more dramatically, by Nietzsche. Andreas-Salomé's originality lay in taking another further step, one epitomized in the crucial concept of "*die Rückwirkung*," or "back-effect."[52] That idea suggests that the images of spirit engendered by the soul—its God or gods—do not remain mere byproducts of practical need and mythic fantasy, but, themselves attaining to a certain critical autonomy vis-a-vis their more personal origins, achieve an authentic mode of spiritual existence capable of entering into dynamic and mutually transformative relationship with the human psyche. So it is that the ideals engendered by the soul's own vision of the best that it can be or hope for take on enduring form as the God—or gods—it reveres. So it is, for instance, that *whether or not* one chooses to believe that the God of the Judeo-Christian tradition exists as a divine and eternal being outside of all time and human history, it simply cannot be denied that His Name and image has exercised—and continues to exercise—inestimable influence upon human culture. Whether or not "God" actually exists ontologically, "He" indubitably does exist as a psychic fact, one virtually all Western human beings (including Richard Dawkins) wrestle with, one way or another.

Such are the first premises of Andreas-Salomé's psychology of religion. Even in this sketchy outline, one can perhaps discern a logic well suited to empower a transformation of the rigid dualisms—or contrary monisms—that characterize the thinking (or lack thereof) of the spirit-soul-body triad in modern times. For Andreas-Salomé's theory manifestly opens an avenue of real communication between (our ideas of) divine spirit and the human soul, teaching, as it does, that the former may be genuinely affected—even transformed—by the latter, and vice versa. Since the possibility of such reciprocal action and mutual effect constitutes the ground of authentic relation, Andreas-Salomé's psychology of religion effectively reestablishes (at least theoretically) a differentiated and so genuine relation between what we have been calling spirit (with the term's inference of divine agency) and the individual human soul; what Rilke, in his *Book of Hours*, addresses as (on the one hand) God and (on the other) his own monkishly creative human self.

This reciprocal and mutually *participatory* relationship between divine and human being qualifies as one of the most striking features of *The Book of Hours.* That it is so striking only illustrates how rigidly and unimaginatively absolutized traditional theology generally is. Knowing full well that we are very imperfect beings and anything but all-powerful, we have immense difficulty getting out of our heads that—whether or not we "believe" in Him— God (the divine) is not *just the opposite:* eternal, finished, perfect, all-powerful and completely self-sufficient. This, after all, is what the Judeo-Christian tradition generally leads us to believe.

Yet Rilke, radical, heretical, Lou-influenced Rilke, tells us otherwise. In the famous sixth poem, our neighbor, God, is like a little child (or a dying parent) that may need to knock so we can bring him a glass full of the water. In the 36th poem, Rilke (or his monk) asks, with concern: "What will you do, God, when I die? . . . Without me what reason do you have?"[53] These radical reversal of the order of dependence are not the whole story. The fifth chapter of *In the Image of Orpheus* discusses at length the full range of dynamic relations between the human self and God enacted in the book, all the various permutations of which merely highlight the essential point: Namely, the divine and human nature, the spirit and the soul, are here involved in mutually participatory creative interrelation.

This is only possible, however, because—while the *Book of Hours* retains the name of God—it *does* radically transform the traditional God-image in many crucial ways, all of which effectively serve to help redress the historic imbalance between spirit, soul, and body that had developed in the course of Western cultural history. For Rilke does not only endeavor to reaffirm the relative autonomy of the human soul vis-a-vis the divine spirit.

That initiative goes hand in glove with a redemption of the value of the created world, the sensible universe. That redemption is effected by his artist-monk's reenvisioning of spirit in the form of a God whose divine substance is, in contrast with orthodox Christian doctrine, *immanent* (one could well say embodied) in the life of the created world, the universe of things. This crucial theme is powerfully present in the very first two poems of the book ("Nothing is too small for me to love" and "I . . . reach out across all things"), but perhaps comes to simplest expression in the 22nd:

> I find you in all these myriad things
> I love and care for like a brother.
> As seed, you sun yourself in the smallest
> and in the greatest, spread generously abroad.
>
> That is the wondrous play of powers
> that move selflessly, upward and down:
> rising in the roots, dwindling in the bough
> and rising like resurrection in the crown.[54]

Or, as Rilke's monk puts it in the 45th poem of the sequence:

For all things
sing you: at times
we just hear them more clearly.[55]

The poem—and in this it follows, again, the central theme so proudly announced in the very first two poems—continues to make clear the crucial function played by the "middle" term, the self or soul, as it holds open the space between the things of the world and their invisible spiritual source, thus making possible the all-important—and all-encompassing—connection between these poles:

Often when I imagine you
your wholeness cascades into many shapes.
You run like a herd of luminous deer
and I am dark, I am forest.[56]

Such instances illustrate that Rilke's God is *both* present in all things and wholly revealed in none because the ground—the origin and source of all—cannot be identified with any particular image or manifestation of it. Rilke's correlative image of divine being as essentially paradoxical ("You are the deepest, who looms tallest/ The diver's and the tower's goal . . . You are the forest of paradox"[57]) and so, a confluence of opposites, reveals an idea of spirit which, while perhaps not perfectly identical with the essence of soul itself (remember that, in the last lecture, we spoke about the gist of soul as a holding of the tension between opposites) is certainly congruent with it; which congruence sanctions a fluid interchange between the substance of spirit, soul, and body. That fluidity in turn arises out of and affirms a different, an inherently symbolic and imaginative relationship to the universe, a stance towards things that is not only an artistic or aesthetic one, but, simultaneously and intrinsically, a religious one as well. And so: a poet as an icon-painting monk, for whom poem, painting, and the religious act of prayer are all one and the same act of psycho-spiritual liberation. Again, the last stanza of the first poem:

> Nothing is too small for me to love
> and paint great on a background of gold.
> I hold it high and know not whose
> soul it will break from the mold.[58]

I would like to finish by foregrounding the dimension that has taken (as is all too commonly the case) something of a back seat in this lecture on the psychology of religion. For it is all very well to speak of a renovation of the prevailing God-image, or employ the concepts of spirit, soul, and body in order to articulate Rilke's—or

Hillman's—attempt to regain a sense of balance of these terms. Yet how is such renovation actually accomplished, performed, effected; what is the medium and milieu in and through which the transformative deed is done?

Rilke's remarkable *Book of Hours* lends us material help in answering this question. It is self-evident that Rilke's vehicle here is, originally and ultimately, the *poetic word.* It is in fact the medium of language itself in and through which the soul reenacts its relation to whatever spiritual ideals it holds and whatever sensible experience it retains in the treasure-house of memory. As in the word *psychology* itself, *logos* and *psyche* are fundamentally inseparable. Soul exists in and through its mode of expression; unfolds its nature, its being, in and through its ongoing embodiment in unique and varied styles of speech.

It would require another entire lecture (at least) to delve into the poetics of Rilke's *Book of Hours*, the formal means by which Rilke shapes his speech so as to effect the spiritual and psychological ends we have been describing, ends that are both envisioned and accomplished in and through the art of the word. In lieu of a more satisfactory exposition, let me call attention to three salient points:

1) In his classic work *The Chinese Written Character as Medium for Poetry,*[59] Ezra Pound observes that poetry

consists of an integral coordination of three essential elements: *phanopoeia, melopoeia, and logopoeia.* The first term derives from the Greek idea that pertains to the power to make something appear (as in the God *Phanes* and the term *phenomenon*) and so relates to poetic *imagery*; the second derives from the Greek term related to melody and music and so refers to the all those poetic elements (including rhythm and tone) that give *voice* to a poem; the last derives from a word that means (among other things) *reason* and refers to the *idea or meaning* of the poem. This may provide one clue as to the original connection between the soul and lyric poetry, for the three terms correspond to the triad of body, soul, and spirit. Insofar as an authentic poem always involves a balanced and integral fusion of the three elements (image, voice, and idea), a differentiated balance of body, soul, and spirit may be understood to be at the core, the heart, of poetry *per se.*

2) Still building upon the line of thought following upon our prior lecture, we could say that what is actually happening or taking place in the lyrics that comprise Rilke's *Book of Hours* is an *enactment* of an (extended) *moment of exchange* or intercourse *between the individual mind or soul* and the realm of spirit or *divine agency*, in connection, too, with the soul's corporeal experience of the world. The vision Rilke embodies in his work is not

Greek, but neither is it exactly Judeo-Christian in any conventional sense. As we've emphasized, Rilke does not imagine "God" as almighty and omniscient, but does envision divine being as *omnipresent,* as both concealed and revealed by all the myriad things of the world. That is to say, the poet's vision of both God and the world transpires under the auspices of *Beauty,* one primary definition of which has always been the seeing of the One in the Many. So it is, again, that the *psychology of religion* at play in Rilke's book is originally and profoundly *aesthetic.*

3) The third point represents the dialectical synthesis of the first two. We have implied (leaning on Lou Andreas-Salomé), that the poet of *The Book of Hours* engenders (his) God in and through the soul's act of creative imagination, the vehicle of which is the poetic word. Yet how do we know that what is thus manifested is not purely subjective? Is not merely some personal fantasy that does not, in fact, truly participate in any more enduring order of things, that more permanent order that has always been the province of the spirit and the realm of any true God?

We know this by virtue of the miracle of *form,* the poetic form in and through which the imaginative inspiration is manifest. By virtue of the shaping power and integrity of form—which constitutes the integral synthesis of image, voice, and meaning—we enter into a transpersonal sphere that cannot be reduced to or contained within the realm of purely personal psychology.

Kathleen Raine tells us, "It is impossible to speak of beauty without speaking of form."[60] She also tells us, "Soul, far from being a vague concept, is on the contrary, the principle of form and the formative principle, which in the human being is the imagination."[61] And finally: "Lyric form is itself the supreme embodiment of archetypal order."[62]

So, by virtue of aesthetic form, *which is connate with the imaginative and shaping activity of the soul,* we participate in the sphere of archetypal intelligence. Poetry thus unfolds the living relation between the archetypal order underlying all things, on the one hand, and, on the other, the sensible percepts that comprise the singularities of embodied experience. Thus is the poetic self, the organ of exchange, never *purely* personal or entirely impersonal. And so—not Rilke, but Rilke's monk—translates his idea of God into the forms of the soul's own embodied experience of itself and its world, *and vice versa.* And so, in reading the poetic prayers that comprise *The Book of Hours* we are not offered mere concepts of God but rather invited to engage in an authentic rite of communion, to partake of the bread of life.

Fourth Lecture

Countering the Cogito – *Esse in Anima*

Worpswede: a small artist colony in the relatively remote North German moorland founded by two landscape painters in 1889. Worpswede: a variegated landscape—at once spacious and intimate—of windblown poplars and birches, silken crops, meandering canals, and the dark water of the surrounding peat bogs that brews the mind as if it were black tea. Worpswede: the locale where a young poet fresh (or not so fresh; in fact, rather exhausted) from the second of two long excursions to Russia meets two young women artists (a painter and a sculptor) whom he calls "sisters in white." Worpswede: a game-changer in the soul history of Rainer Maria Rilke.

Rilke's initial stay in Worpswede was relatively brief: six weeks. Why, and how, did that short stint prove such a pivotal episode in the evolution of his consciousness, the soul story we are trying to tell? The answer to that question—like most all pertaining to the soul—is complex and ambiguous, if not downright paradoxical. On the one hand, one could truly say that the actuality of Rilke's experience at Worpswede *changed everything*; that it dramatically altered his angle of vision and transmuted the very terms in which he perceived the world. On the other, one could say, with equal validity, that what Worpswede signified for Rilke could be regarded as the logical consequence and natural continuation of all that had gone before, especially his liaison with Lou and formative journeys to Italy and Russia.

With respect to that first perspective, we might put the matter thus: In the preceding chapter (or—cf. his *Visions of Christ*—chapters) of Rilke's life, religion played a dominant role. By religion here I mean not only the spiritual inclination we might (with Jung or Andreas-Salomé) call the religious instinct or affect, but the officially recognized language of religion, those forms, practices and phrases long identified with the Abrahamic religions of the Book: Judaism, Christianity, and (cf. Chapter Five of the *Soul History*) Islam. Thus, *The Book of Monastic Life* was originally called, simply, *Prayers*, and it unfolds as a dialogue between a monk who speaks as the first person, the "I" of the poem, and his God, the (one) divine being explicitly named and addressed as such. The poem thus revolves around the center of the "I-Thou" relationship sustained between a religious personage and (his) God.

With Rilke's move to Worpswede, the vocabulary he employs to address matters of the spirit alters drastically. As the *Soul History* notes, "very few poems in or immediately after Worpswede possess obvious religious content, and Rilke mentions God only three or four times in the almost one hundred pages of prose in his diary devoted to his Worpswede stay."[63] The only substantial such entry is the last composed in Worpswede, which transcribes a discussion between Rilke and one of those two "sisters in white"—Paula Becker. Rilke, writing in Paula Becker's own voice, reports:

> "When you were first here I so often marveled that you (Rilke) used the name God . . . and that you were able to use it so beautifully. I myself was totally without that word. It's true I never felt any great need for it either. There were times, earlier, when I believed: he is in the wind, but for the most part I didn't experience him as a unified personality at all . . . I knew only aspects of God. And many of those aspects were horrifying . . . All the same it would be comforting to believe in a personality around

> whom all circles close, a mountain of power before whom all people and all countries of all people lie open . . ." And later on [in our conversation]: "No, it would all be foreign doctrine, for me God will always be 'she, Nature.'"[64]

These are Paula Becker's sentiments, not necessarily Rilke's own. The poet, as he tells us, "argued on his (God's) behalf." Even so, the literary evidence indicates that Rilke in fact took his friend's view very much to heart, a conclusion congruent with the general truth that the gist of Rilke's Worpswede experience consisted in large part in understanding and assimilating the way of seeing and being embodied by Paula and Clara, the two "sisters in white." So it is that—in writing the formula of Rilke's new religious life—it would not be inaccurate to follow Paula's lead and, on the one side, scratch "God" and replace Him with (as Paula would have it): "she, Nature."

Another passage from Rilke's diary reveals that the other, first side of the "I-Thou" equation—the nature of the poet's own *self*-consciousness—suffers no less of a sea change in the transition from Russia to Worpswede. The relevant entry is especially significant in this regard because it explicitly contrasts Rilke's Worpswede frame of mind with the psychology that, in his own view, characterized Rilke's Russian expedition (referred to here as "the grand tour"). Rilke, remarking upon the nature in and around Worpswede, writes:

> I place great trust in this landscape and will gladly accept from it path and possibilities for many days. Here I can once again simply go along, become, be someone who changes. On the grand tour it was a great burden to have to be someone who is firm, someone who stands, someone who remains immovable in the face of the profusely fleeting, the always unexpected.[65]

A related passage amplifies these same themes:

> There is something like selflessness in this way of taking part in nature. I am gradually beginning to comprehend this life that passes through large eyes into eternally waiting souls. This daily attentiveness, alertness, and eagerness of the senses turned outward, this thousandfold seeing and seeing always away from oneself, this not-accompanying-oneself in the changing landscape with one's looks, this being only eye, without having to justify over whom.—This

> purity of life, this always being joyful because something always is happening, not that it has any bearing on one's own personality, but simply that there is motion and change.[66]

So much, one might say, for the quasi-Romantic self-consciousness—the rather self-celebratory "I"—Rilke acquired in Italy and which found such clear expression in *The Book of Monastic Life.* This prose passage speaks in a tone of voice dramatically different from—indeed diametrically opposed to—that which proudly proclaimed: "Nothing was whole before I beheld it/all becoming stands still." True, Russia itself in some wise represented, too, the self-effacing side of Rilke's religious affect, but Worpswede does so in a new guise, a manner reflecting not so much the *humility* of the reverential *self* as the *lability* of the selfless soul, the mutability inherent in its nature as a mirrorlike receptacle of being.

It is, of course, no accident that this last-cited passage, like the conversation with Paula Becker about God, describes a mode of consciousness represented by one or both of "the sisters in white," Rilke's young women- or girl-friends. It is no surprise, because Worpswede, for Rilke, was all about—not God and the ego-consciousness made in His image (or, *a lá* Lou Andreas-Salomé's psychology of religion, vice versa)— but *"she, Nature"* and the psychic reflection of that ever-changeful state of (non-)being called, by Jung and Hillman, *anima.* And that implies a revisioning of the very idea of the mode of consciousness—or unconsciousness!—we might consider as normative of the human being, most deeply and authentically characteristic of the essential nature of the psyche itself.

Now what this means within the context of our ongoing intellectual historical discussion is, in the first place, that the categories of spirit, soul, and body are rendered less rigid and more fluid. As long as a traditional religious vocabulary is employed, it is relatively easy to identify Spirit with God, the body with Nature or the physical world, and the Soul with the "I" in-between—even if, as we have seen, a dualistic construction of spirit and matter opens a trapdoor under that middle term and sends it spinning into the "abyss of Self." But if the place of God—and so Spirit—is taken by "she, Nature"; and the self or "I" does not so much aspire to ascend to the realm of God in Heaven or realize His image here on earth but rather tends to elide itself in order better to reflect an ever-changing natural reality . . . well, then, these categories become rather confused, don't they? For then, our notions of spirit, soul, and body start running one into the other in such a way as to make the drawing of clear lines between them problematical—as if they were in fact all actually mere *modulations* of *one and the same unific essence* rather than totally distinct kinds of being.

But perhaps this sort of "confusion" is not so much chaotic as it is a new, deeper kind of order emerging out of a vision (associated, *a lá* Hillman, with a soul-centered psychology) that does indeed repudiate overly rigid divisions between (e.g.) God and Nature or the divine Christ and the human soul—a soul traditionally supposed to be steeped in original sin on account of Eve's (her, Nature's) primordial transgression.

Here we may note that the epochal shift we are hinting at (one associated with the obsolescence of *both* the transcendent monism of dominant strains of Christianity *and* the materialistic monism of modern science), this critical loosening of the metaphysical opposition of spirit and matter, had (as far as the soul history of our poet is concerned) already been initiated by *The Book of Hours.* As we've noted, that book is anything *but* orthodox in its religious views. We might say, in fact, that the traditional metaphysical and religious structures loosened in that work are, in Worpswede, shaken free of that scaffolding altogether; might imagine that the restless winds frequently blowing through the vast moorland *unhinge* Rilke's vision from its time-honored dedication to the name of God and, too, an historic attachment to more masculine inflections of ego or self-consciousness. That detachment, in turn, liberates him to learn deeper lessons about the true (and truly fathomless) nature of the soul itself by observing (and falling more than a little bit in love with) the soul qua anima or (to employ Paula's own compound term) "she, Nature."

This then may qualify as a nod in the direction of that *second* perspective alluded to earlier, that viewpoint from which we could comprehend Worpswede as, not the contradiction, but the natural continuation of Rilke's prior life and work.

Even so, it is worth marking again the substitution of terms, for in Worpswede, Rilke no longer feels the need to signify his concern with spirituality by patently religious symbolism. He no longer needs his exemplary artist to be an officially religious personage (a monk). That would, in fact, get in the way of his evolving (or should we rather say *in*volving) angle of vision. In this new chapter of life, it is better—far better—for that exemplary artist to be no monk, but a young woman who is, in her innermost essence, not only an artist but *a maiden consciousness,* a girl, and so a visible embodiment of self (or selflessness!) as *soul qua anima.*[67]

Very well, but how are we to gain approach to a surer understanding of—or, better, engagement with—that mysterious essence of soul called anima? Read Hillman, read Jung, fall in love—all these can help . . . or hurt. But in these few pages, the best we can do is continue to read Rilke and at least one depth psychologist who shares a kindred poetic sensibility.

Another passage from Rilke's journal—even while confirming that our still monkish poet wasn't much of a partygoer—deliberately probes the deep nature of anima consciousness as such is exemplified, in Rilke's mind, by Paula and Clara:

> *[After a Sunday evening gathering at the Barkenhoff that was ending with . . .]* jokes, clowning, sickening end of German conviviality. But the ending was beautiful in spite of it all, and it was the girls in white who redeemed it. I opened the door to my room which was growing cold and dark blue like a grotto. I pushed open my window, and then they came to join the miracle and leaned out brightly into the moonlit night, which enveloped their laughter-hot cheeks in cold. And suddenly they all became so poignant in their gazing. Half fully aware, i.e. as painters, half intuitively, i.e. as girls. Initially the mood seized them, the single note of this misty night with its almost full moon over the three poplar trees, this mood of faintly

> tarnished silver robs them of their defenses and forces them into the dark, yearning-filled life of girls . . . Then the artist in them gains control and gazes and gazes, and when the artist has become deep enough in this gazing, they are once more at the threshold of their own being and miracle and glide gently back into their life as girls. That's why they always gaze so long into the landscape.[68]

This is a beautiful evocation of the subtle dynamic of exchange between the human soul and nature, the soul and (the body of) the world intrinsic to *anima.* That dynamic finds analogous expression in a passage by Robert Romanyshyn, a depth psychologist particularly well-attuned to the poetic sensibility inherent in anima-consciousness. The following is from Romanyshyn's essay "Yes, Indeed! Do Call the World the Vale of Soul Making":

> Gaston Bachelard, the great French master of reverie, says that poetry helps one breathe better. This claim is not just extravagant nonsense, a mere aesthetic diversion. Something of great value is present in these words, something we have lost, something we no longer remember

> of ourselves and about our place within the order of creation. Breath is life; it is soul, the anima mundi. When we breathe we exchange ourselves with the world around us. On the in-breath, in the moment of inspiration, we not only take in the world, we are also nourished by it, in-spired by it. And then at the pause, so slight and so subtle, in that briefest of moments before the ex-piration, when we give back to the world what it has just given to us, an alchemy occurs. Sound becomes word, rhythm becomes song, and the world blossoms into a new kind of beauty. On a bit of moving air, on this so fragile, slender, invisible thread depends the continuing act of creation.[69]

A couple of preliminary remarks on this passage. Firstly, it is certainly no accident that the passage begins by citing Gaston Bachelard. Bachelard's book *The Poetics of Reverie*[70]—a classic that inspires much of Romanyshyn's own work—unfolds a worldview explicitly centered in the *contemplative* mode of consciousness characteristic of the deepest strata of the feminine registers of the soul. Secondly, the affinity between Romanyshyn's and Rilke's evocations is remarkable. Romanyshyn, in fact, continues his essay with a discussion of Rilke, albeit not the Rilke passage cited here, but lines from the *Duino Elegies*. We'll come to the *Elegies* later in this course; for now, let's allow ourselves time to linger upon the two sister citations we've quoted here and contemplate their resonant implications.

The passages accord so deeply with each other because, while one revolves around the sense of sight and the other around that of breath and sound, both evoke a process of vital interchange between the soul and the world. That subtle reciprocal dynamic does *not* leave the Cartesian ego intact and in control as the indubitable locus of human identity but rather decenters that historically dominant egocentric perspective. Let's review, for a moment, the constitution of the Cartesian subject so as to better see how Rilke and Romanyshyn both offer a quite different model of identity, one in accord *not* with the famous *cogito ergo sum* but with the competing dictum favored by Jung: *esse in anima*, "being in soul."

Descartes, you will recall, found that he could doubt the existence of anything and everything *except* the operation of his own mind as it formulated and deliberated the question of existence. The Cartesian ego is thus originally constituted by an *exclusion* of all that is foreign to its own cognitive reflexivity; any and all contents of consciousness *except* that of its image of itself generating thought. Cartesian consciousness, like Augustinian theology, thus originates in an *aversion* to the world—a turning away from all that is given in and through bodily sensation, and that means, too, all that cannot be immediately and certainly known by a self-reflexive act of cognition. That amounts to the entire mystery of existence as such appears extrinsic to the subject's own self-conception.

By way of contrast, let us look at the scenario Rilke records in his journal and read it as a kind of parable of the origination of a quite different—intrinsically poetic or aesthetic—mode of soul consciousness. We might begin by construing the party at the Barkenhoff as a scene wherein Rilke (our representative man) finds himself disoriented and indeed largely lost amid a sea of disparate sense impressions, a conventional social reality devoid of the space and time required for meaningful self-reflection. Consequently, Rilke removes himself from the (to him) uncongenial setting and retreats to his room. The poet in his room—in the enclosed space that is (for now, anyway) his own and which holds him within its impermeable walls . . . is this not a symbol of his own self-contained identity; the bounds of his "I" or ego-consciousness? As such, it is, in one aspect at least, a site of refuge and indeed defense against all that is rejected as, not only *not* the self, but irrelevant to it.

And yet it is more than that as well.

In her book *Pregnant Darkness*, Monika Wikman tells us that "it is the very nature of the ego functioning to defend against the dynamic fluidity of the psyche and the mysteries of which we are all a part."[71] Rilke does retreat to remove himself from a sphere of what he regards as disorderly sensation, but his room does not remain solely a place of reflexive self-withdrawal, for that enclosed space does have a kind of life of its own. Indeed, in the course of Rilke's own pregnant description, the room itself takes on alchemical resonance as it grows "cold and dark like a grotto" and becomes—no sterile petri dish in which a scientifically controlled experiment of consciousness may be conducted—but a container, an empty vessel full of the possibility of transformation.

For Rilke, our poet, does *not* want—and cannot afford—to ward off "the dynamic fluidity of the psyche" and the larger mysteries of which we are a part. And so, he voluntarily breaches the boundary of his self-contained identity by opening the door to his room and letting in "the girls"—Paula and Clara, the sisters in white, the bearers of anima consciousness. Indeed, our poet does still more, far more, than that, for he intuitively knows that the soul cannot live and grow within the suffocating confines of a space closed off to external nature; that it needs fresh air to breathe. So, Rilke, immediately and instinctively, throws open the window of his room so that girls might breathe the fresh air and—gazing in reverie out into (no sunlit day but) the moonlit night—receive into themselves something of the mysteries of the cosmos. There, on the sill of the poet's room (remember the threshold in *Entrance*, the poem that served as portal to these lectures), the poet-alchemist's mystic sisters breathe in and . . .

> . . . then, at the pause, so slight and so subtle, in that briefest of moments before the ex-piration, when we give back to the world what it has just given to us, an alchemy occurs. Sound becomes word, rhythm becomes song . . .

> . . . *Halb Unbewußtes leben, halb im Eifer*
> *feststellen, was man schaute, wie and wo,*
> *zu Zielen gehn und wieder dann ein Streifer*
> *im Ungewissen werden, einsam froh—:*
> *hier leben diese schönen Mädchen so, -*
> *halb noch ergriffen, sind sie schon Ergreifer . . .*[72]

This poem—or poetic fragment—represents Rilke's lyrical rendition of the scene he painted in prose. You will find the English translation in the *Soul History,*[73] but for now I wanted us merely to listen, to hear the sounds of words as they themselves participate in the rhythm of life, as they lift into song. All Rilke's poems flow from a similar place of origin, an analogous primal scene: no Cartesian subject abstracting himself from the pregnant mysteries of the world, but a poetic identity opening its internal space to the incursions—and excursions— of soul and so to the way anima consciousness naturally flows alternately out into the world and back into its own fathomless depths, building, crossing, and recrossing a bridge between present actuality and the beyond, conscious identity and unconscious mystery, personal reality and the archetypal images nested in nature, the *anima mundi,* or soul of the world, of which the individual soul is a continuous part. Nor can that steady, rhythmic breathing, that continual crossing, ever be comprehended or commandeered by concept-ridden ego-consciousness alone, for such movement is of the essence of creative imagination. "Only girls," writes Rilke, "do not ask/ What bridges leads to images"[74]—those poetic images and painterly songs that (as Romanyshyn puts it) adorn creation with "a new kind of beauty."

Let us then briefly summarize—theoretically—the difference between the mode of consciousness derivative of the *ego cogito* and that of *esse in anima.*

It is not that the girls (who are not only painters but artists, and so, too, exemplars of *poetic* consciousness;

otherwise, why would Rilke consider them so deeply?) do not think; nor do they cease entirely to exist as centers of consciousness, as distinct identities. But they do think differently and embody a different form of existence. Rather than their consciousness forming and fixing itself as clear and distinctly defined subjects over against external objects, their subjectivity takes shape, originally and primordially, in *relationship* to a world experienced as provisionally, but not finally, other; in, that is, an openness to pregnant mystery that implies a dissolution of any rigid boundary of the self. This does not entail an existential annihilation of selfhood as such, for—after this openness invites an inflow of sensation—the girls' (or the poet's) consciousness reasserts its active energy, and its capacity in turn to recreate its own image of the sensations it has received. Poetic consciousness, qua soul or anima consciousness, thus functions as a locus of transformative relation and imaginative mediation, the node of a dynamic of reception and generation that depends upon an oscillation between knowing and unknowing, conscious and unconscious modes of being and nonbeing.

After centuries dominated by the cognitive function of the ego, perhaps Romanyshyn may be all too literally correct when he suggests that our continued survival may hinge upon our ability to transform our idea of who and what we are by opening the space of our conscious identity to the animating intelligence of those soul figures—those sisters in white—that have the power to reanimate our life and our love. The frenetic pace of the whirling material and sociopolitical world to the contrary, so much does after all depend upon "a bit of moving air, on this so fragile, slender, invisible thread" of the poetic sensibility that is the thought of the heart.

Fifth Lecture

The Eye of the Panther

Today, for this lecture—the first of the second half of this course—I want to take up themes sounded in the piece that is bound in book form with *The Thought of the Heart,* the Hillmanian discourse that provided our theoretical point of departure. *Anima Mundi: The Return of the Soul to the World*[75] not only develops the aesthetic plot hatched in *The Thought of the Heart,* its very title bespeaks its underlying continuity with the subject of our last lecture. And so today it will be our task to elaborate the connection between *anima* as a mode of contemplative awareness and imaginative activity (as illustrated by Rilke's portrait of Paula and Clara) and its broader significance in the form of the *anima mundi* or soul of the world.

The association between our previous discussion and Hillman's *Anima Mundi* goes well past mere titular resonance, for the philosophical issues addressed in our prior comparison of the *ego cogito sum* and *esse in anima* supply the metaphysical ground of the revisioning of psychology Hillman advocates in this (as well as other) major work. That revisioning aims (among other things) to expose *psychology's own unconscious investment in the metaphysical dualism* (or dueling monisms) characteristic of the worldview that has dominated Western thought for centuries. We can initiate our exploration of this topos by placing the particular argument that Hillman makes in *The Return of the Soul to the World* within the intellectual historical frame of reference we have repeatedly re- (and de-)constructed.

In *Anima Mundi,* Hillman pointedly criticizes the field of psychology's endemic tendency to view the soul as—exclusively—the *human subject* as such exists vis-a-vis an objective world construed as essentially soulless. Citing the persistence of "the idea of the external world passed to us by Aquinas, Descartes, Locke, and Kant," Hillman writes:

> Precisely this external, non-subjective view of the world now needs to be reworked.

Before we proceed with it, we have first to recollect the idea of reality which generally operates throughout depth psychology. Psychological dictionaries and schools of all orientations agree that reality is of two kinds.

First, the word means the totality of existing material objects or the sum of conditions of the external world . . . Second, there is a psychic reality, not extended in space, the realm of private experience that is interior, wishful, imaginational. Having divided psychic reality from hard or external reality, psychology elaborates various theories to connect the two orders together, since the division is worrisome indeed. It means that psychic reality is conceived to be neither public, objective, nor physical, while external reality . . . is conceived to be utterly devoid of soul. As the soul is without world, so the world is without soul.

Therefore when something goes wrong in life, depth psychology still looks to intra- and intersubjectivity for the cause and the therapy. The public, objective, physical world of things . . . is by definition excluded from psychological etiology and therapy. *Things lie outside the soul.*[76]

This is clear enough. What could, however, be filled in somewhat is the backstory behind psychology's assumption of this position and the weighty historical reasons for its intransigent attachment to it.

We have already related part of this story. The field of psychology we recognize as such today emerged in the mid- to late 19th century and matured in the early 20th. Its initial, formative period coincided with the intensification (I have previously called it the *absolutizing*) of the already operative metaphysical split between spirit and matter, a development catalyzed by Darwin and finding cultural expression in a decisive widening of the divide between religion and science. Neither the split between spirit and matter nor that between science and religion was new. Nonetheless, before Darwin published his theory of evolution, modern science had as yet to extend, by way of the systematic method proper to it, its doctrine of materialism to, not only the physiology of life (Harvey had done a good deal in that direction), but the *genesis and development of being—including and indeed especially human being—itself.* What Darwin effectively did was thus to expand the reach of mechanistic theory into the first and last refuge of religion: namely, *creation mythology,* the narratives that generate our primal images of the origin and nature of *human being and consciousness per se* as such finds its appointed place in the cosmos.

In so doing, Darwin dealt God—for centuries, the accepted standard-bearer of the soul's religious instinct—a death blow, a knockout duly announced by Nietzsche.

Even in its moment of triumph, however, science could never claim complete and total victory. Science, while largely vanquishing religion, did not succeed in extinguishing all traces of the idea of God; could not manage to collapse the reigning spirit-matter dualism into a materialistic monism entirely—without, that is, leaving significant historical residue. Such a deed, if actually executed, would after all annihilate not only the name of God but all facets of spirit traditionally carried by myth and religion, including all ideas of goodness, meaning, purpose, order, and indeed the soul of human consciousness (or: the human consciousness of soul) itself.

Do not get me wrong: One current of the intellectual mainstream indeed flowed—and still flows with abominable power—in just this robotic direction. We are all, here and now (as any number of dystopic films will attest), fighting to keep from being swept into oblivion by just this terrible torrent. It is true, too, that that stream of psychological thought that overidentifies with science continues to contribute its own relatively puny force to that mighty current.

Fortunately, this is not the whole story. For another current of psychological reflection remained committed to the deeper idea of soul and intelligently dedicated to serving its inherent desire for spiritual sustenance and meaning. Even so, this countercurrrent could not depend upon a discredited God to supply that end. Indeed, as Jung suggested, psychology itself arose, in significant measure, precisely because religion could no longer fulfill that paramount need and a new cultural initiative that might fill the tremendous spiritual vacuum thus created was called for—desperately called for—by the larger order of things, by the collective psyche or Spirit of the Times.

And so, psychology did step in to fill that vacuum, but its (politically necessary) indenture to science meant that it could do so only while maintaining the spirit-matter dualism inherent to the scientific worldview largely intact. Consequently, within the precincts of psychology, the spiritual values traditionally associated with God were swallowed, more or less whole, by what seemed—since Descartes and after Darwin—the only sure refuge of consciousness, intelligence, and authentic identity: the human subject in its godlike capacities of thought and reflexive self-awareness *as this subject defines itself—*

in the image of the God it replaces—over against an external world devoid of such admirable soul-spiritual qualities. Thus, still functioning within the frame of an essentially untransformed spirit-matter dualism, the human psyche absorbed into its own subjective sphere the full weight of religious meaning traditionally born by God or (in a more Greek inflection) universal ideas of cosmic order and meaning.

Well, that kind of worked, maybe, for a while . . . didn't it?

Look at the mess we are in, shouts James Hillman, our own homegrown prophet of the soul, crying in the wilderness of the modern world. That very ego- and anthropocentric psychology has, he claims, colluded with the destructive tendencies of our mainstream philosophic and scientific tradition by denying the world soul and cutting our soul off from the world. No matter if we live in our dreams or carefully unfold the intricate origami of our inner lives, if we leave the world out of the picture, we are not doing it—or ourselves—justice and will soon run out of imaginative steam and the inspiration that nourishes the soul's creative life. It is time, Hillman tells us, to begin paying the interest due on our century-old investment in the self. That we will be much the richer for it is not even the chief point. This reorientation is, at this juncture, a matter of physical as well as spiritual survival.

How then do we go about more fully understanding and (this is what really matters) making that shift, transforming (our idea of) ourselves and our world so as to give the world back to the soul and return soul to the world?

Well, for one thing, we can continue what we have been doing here: reading Rilke. For the ground we have covered so far—the trajectory of the poet's own soul-making—tends in just this direction as it leads us from his time and place of birth and early influences (beginning, for instance, with his Catholic upbringing) toward his more mature poetic vision, the gist of which is the realization of just this epochal shift.

We imagine that the period of prophecy lies in the distant past, with Elijah, John the Baptist, or Mohammed, but that is a weak-minded, faint-hearted notion utterly at odds with the teachings of America's own great spokesperson, Ralph Waldo Emerson. Rilke (who read Emerson) should himself be leagued with that school of poet-prophets the critic Harold Bloom so aptly called "the visionary company."[77] Bloom employed the term to refer to the English Romantic poets, many of whom evince intense self-consciousness of the hallowed role of the Bard ("So prayed, more gaining than he asked, the Bard/In holiest mood" writes Wordsworth in the *Prospectus* to his fragmentary epic, *The Excursion*[78]). Rilke gets there, too, as we'll see, in his thunderous *Duino Elegies,* although our more modern poet sings his song in a different, darker register. What I wish to stress here, however, is that each way station of Rilke's soul journey represents a step on that prophetic path: his *Christ Visions*, his *Book of Hours*, and now the work that brings to poetic fruition the new, anima-infused inspiration seeded in Worpswede: his *New Poems.*

To be sure, the voice that speaks the *New Poems* does not sound particularly prophetic—much less so, in fact, than the religious one that offers such soaring prayers in *The Book of Hours.* Indeed, far from trumpeting a new revelation from the confident center of a vatic "I" ("I sing myself, and celebrate myself"—Whitman[79]), Rilke's self rather seems to disappear altogether in the body of his *New Poems,* which, rather than presenting any grand brand-new spiritual vision, appears simply to be a collection giving voice to the many and diverse things of the world.

Yet it is, of course, just this that embodies the transformative—even visionary—force of the book. Because in the *New Poems* it is not the human self qua "I" or ego that is the chief *subject* (and I repeat: *subject*) of the work—the center of interest that speaks to us—

but rather *the world itself.* I mean that external ("public, objective, physical") world of *things* that, as Hillman says in the last line of the quoted passage, "lie outside the soul." Except that here, in Rilke's Paris, they don't. For our poet's is a living, speaking world, a multifaceted reality displaying here *this* and there *that* face or feature, a constantly stirring world of animated sign and meaningful gesture; in short and sum, a world ensouled. And so, the sense of spirit, the name of the divinity at work in this world is not the one God, but the pleromatic *Anima Mundi.*

The poetic consciousness engendering the ensouled world of the *New Poems* follows as a logical extension of the anima consciousness Rilke cultivated in Worpswede. The soul itself, no longer dominated by or in service to any fixed egoic identity, is free to flow out into manifestation in order to see what it can find there and—by virtue of the imaginative capacity, the thought of the heart that is its soul essence—find, too, the means of reflecting that found reality (which, in truth, is nothing *other* than itself) in the forms of its own creative activity—*Voila!* Rilke's *New Poems,* which are *new* not only in the trivial sense of not having been written before but in the sense that they represent a new way of seeing and being, a new world of existence smack in the middle of Paris, the veritable heart of the old one.

How can we be so sure, so positive about all this? Let's go back to Hillman, who is very clear and precise about the nature of this new, this reenvisioned landscape that is intrinsically both inside and outside, psychological and sensible at one and the same time:

> Let us imagine the *anima mundi* neither above the world encircling it as a divine and remote emanation of spirit, a world of powers, archetypes, and principles transcendent to things, nor within the material world as its unifying panpsychic life-principle. Rather let us imagine the *anima mundi* as that particular soul-spark, that seminal image, which offers itself through each thing in its visible form. Then *anima mundi* indicates the animated possibilities presented by each event as it is, its sensuous presentation as a face bespeaking its interior image—in short, its availability to imagination, its presence as a psychic *reality.* Not only animals and plants ensouled as in the Romantic vision, but soul is given with each thing, God-given things of nature and man-made things of the street.[80]

Read or reread this (and the next two Hillman pages that amplify this insight) carefully, and then read or reread, Rilke's *New Poems*, and you will surely *see* what I mean. The translation is flawless, picture-perfect. In his *New Poems,* Rilke *does* precisely what Hillman *says;* realizes Hillman's prescription—not conceptually or theoretically but practically speaking, as a way of being-in-the-world.

And how does he do so, what is the medium of this translation from idea to embodied fact of life? The very terms of Hillman's program determine it as essentially *aesthetic;* it involves "moving . . . the seat of the soul from brain to heart and the method of psychology from cognitive understanding to aesthetic sensitivity."[81] Further: "The move to the heart is already a move of *poeisis:* metaphorical, psychological."[82]

All this our poet intuitively understands. The natural medium of translation doubles as the language of his art: the poetic word, the imaginative speech of the soul.

We've already encountered one particularly powerful—and poignant—example of Rilke's poetic praxis in *The Panther.*

I say powerful because wild cats—lions, tigers (think Blake), and panthers—have always served as potent archetypal symbols of the sheer power, and terrible beauty, of *anima mundi*, the wild, primal, potentially killing energy that cannot really be tamed or controlled by man. Such an unconquerable will-force[83] is of the essence of the thing we name "Panther," that defining essence that Neoplatonism would call the *logos* or idea of the thing and which Hillman calls the "soul spark or seminal image." The magic of Rilke's art is that he does not only see that scintillating idea, but—like the supple statue of a panther by Rodin's teacher Antoine-Louis Barye that first set that great sculptor on his path—he effectively recreates it in the sinewy syntax, fluidly articulated rhythm and vivid imagery of his poem:

THE PANTHER

The passing of the bars fatigues his gaze
so much, that it can hold no more.
To him it is as if each bar were a maze
that led to another and another barred door.

The quiet pacing of the strong and supple limbs
that turn around the very smallest sphere
is like a dance of power around the rims
of circles, that hold a great will numb in there.

Only seldom does the pupil's curtain slide
soundlessly up—. Then an image enters,
ripples through the tensely stilled stride
and ceases where the rhythm centers.[84]

I say poignant because, even as the poem shows the idea of the thing as it embodies the wild beauty of *anima mundi*, it simultaneously represents its negation. For Rilke shows the panther *caged* and so *not* free to be what it, in essence, is; incapable of realizing its true nature. And so, the image of the world—its world—that would live and blossom in the panther's heart instead . . . dies there, just as the world-image has died, and keeps dying, over and over again, in the prison of ego-subjectivity that cages our own human soul. And so, in creating an image of the thing in the world—the Panther—the poet simultaneously sees into something of the essence of the human soul. "Inside" and "outside"—no less than spirit and matter—are revealed as artificial divisions, rigid dualisms that function as the bars of our own cage, killing the thought of the heart.

All the things in Rilke's book, animate or inanimate, "real" or "imagined," exhibit this same kind of speaking face. They do not remain on the page, or in the world, as inanimate objects or things but are made to appear as possessing (inherently, in and of themselves) soul qualities which it is their nature to display. The poet's art manifests them as forms of *psychic* existences. Thus, when we are introduced, in the very first lines of the very first poem,[85] to the statue of Apollo, the figure is not presented as a stone artifact. Rather, the statue *is* the god, whose luminous gaze is likened to the light of morning shining through still leafless branches in a bright and radiant spring. When we bear witness to the ripples spreading and water spilling into the sequent basins of a Roman fountain, we see no dead object or play of merely physical elements, but an ensouled presence "laughing with transitions." The relevant instances are virtually infinite, for, just as it is nigh impossible to find a surface on a Rodin statue that looks lifeless, unanimated by a vital current, so is it vain to search for lines in Rilke's *New Poems* that do not communicate this sense of abiding, stirring, transfiguring soul.

And so, the poet bears witness—a quiet, anima-inspired, relatively self- or ego-less yet nonetheless inspired and even prophetic witness—to *anima mundi,* the soul of the world.

And this way of seeing (inseparably psychological and aesthetic, metaphoric and poetic, perceptive and creatively imaginative) Hillman calls "personifying." It is the first, and arguably most basic, mode of soul-making introduced in his seminal work, *Revisioning Psychology.* Mythically speaking, it is also (as discussed in *In the Image of Orpheus*) the gist, the heart, the educative kernel of Psyche's first labor, the first major step on her long path toward reunion with Love.

Psyche's labors commence in the aftermath of the deep, life-threatening *nigredo* she suffers after she (at her sister's urging) lights the oil lamp so as to discover the identity of her secret lover; pricks her finger on Eros's arrow and falls in love with the sleeping God all over again; mistakenly spills hot oil on him and is devastated when he—wounded by her betrayal as well as the searing oil—flies away. We have not, in these talks, addressed that pivotal nigredo, the alchemical ground of the transformative imaginative work essayed in the ensuing labors, but will do so in connection with Rilke's later works, including Rilke's novel *The Notebooks of Malte Laurids Brigge.*[86] In accord with the usual order of alchemical process, the psychological and literary origins of *The Notebooks* (Rilke's initial disorientation in urban Paris and his letters detailing the same) actually predate the *New Poems.*

For now, though, let us finish by lending attention to Psyche's labors: beginning—as is only natural—with the first.

While Rilke's masterful *New Poems* make that first labor look rather easy, it is, of course, anything but. Rilke underwent a multiyear artistic apprenticeship under the tutelage of the sculptor August Rodin before he could write the *New Poems*, a breakthrough work that miraculously translates Rodin's sculptural aesthetic into the dramatically different medium of poetic language. If anyone thinks writing something like one of Rilke's *New Poems* doesn't pose too much of a challenge, I suggest you go ahead and try your hand at it. I expect you will quickly find that, on the contrary, it may well seem (like the task of getting that whole confused mass of different seeds sorted and in order) virtually impossible.

True, Rilke's *New Poems* represents an extra-ordinarily complex and deeply developed form of personifying, and one should by no means imagine that one can only engage in this first indispensable mode of soul-making only upon attaining a like degree of imaginative mastery. If our involvement with our world is at all alive and vital, we are assuredly personifying one way or another to a greater or lesser degree. Even so, that matter of degree is no small one, and it would be counterproductive and even dangerous to underestimate the spiritual and imaginative challenge represented by Psyche's labors, this first one as well as all that follow. Looking at those labors within the larger context of the myth as a whole, its cast of characters and defining plot, can deepen our understanding of the true magnitude of trial and travail symbolized by these mythical tasks.

First, let us acknowledge this primary truth: Even while we have been endeavoring to deconstruct the metaphysical divide between spirit and matter and, correlatively, between the divine and earthly or immortal and mortal realms of being, no bridging of that gap ever *closes* it entirely. Archetypal psychology may well argue that in this, our era, the gods are within us, but this should not be taken to mean that the mortal psyche can, without further ado or dire consequence, carelessly identify its own uninitiated consciousness with that of the numinous archetypal powers that comprise its divine ground. Hillman's psychology certainly does *not* endorse conflating the archetypal powers we call "the gods" with the human-all-too-human consciousness of the average—or even above average—ego. On the contrary! No friend at all of what he dismissively calls "humanistic psychology," Hillman, in the last chapter of *Revisioning*, virtually identifies soul-making itself—the crux of his psychology—with a process he calls "dehumanizing." That may well be a rather off-putting and, I would argue, potentially misleading term, but before we could begin to criticize it, we had better understand what it might mean and why Hillman chose it in the first place.

The myth helps. For this we can be sure of: At the start of the tale, Psyche is certainly human. Extraordinary and radiantly beautiful as she may be, she is nonetheless decidedly a mortal human being. We know this for sure because the myth makes much of the difference in kind between Psyche and the Goddess of Beauty herself,

Aphrodite, who becomes incensed precisely because people begin worshipping the mortal Psyche as if she were in fact divine, a goddess like herself. Significantly enough, that confusion or conflation is analogous to the one we described, near the beginning of this lecture, as characteristic of the emergent field of psychology itself, although in that context, the god in question is not Aphrodite but Yahweh.

In any event, Psyche is lucky (or cursed!) enough eventually to become beloved of another god, Aphrodite's son, Eros. And, initially, the only way that the mortal Psyche can have and sustain intercourse with archetypal Eros, the God of Love himself, is in that fairy- tale phase when she has no idea, really, of who he is and is quite unconscious of—not only of the identity of the god—but of her own as well.

Not that we are likely to be much better off, for who among us truly knows what it really means to be Psyche, the human soul?

In that initial, as yet uninitiated state, while she can, for a while, unconsciously play the beloved of Eros, Psyche is in no condition to become his wife or partner, for she is nowhere near anything like his equal. Of course, we may well ask: Can the human psyche ever close the gap between its own being and divine nature? Is there ever any possibility of real relationship between mortal and immortal, the most personal and numinously archetypal registers of life and mind?

Let us pause and breathe for a moment, for we are indeed entering deep waters here. What I have been speaking of above, what I have been saying about the difference between the mortal psyche and divine nature—well, these are not just words. If you've ever had a truly numinous experience, you may well have some concrete idea, some living sense of what I mean. There are, of course, various degrees and kinds of such experience: the awe one may feel in gazing (as Romantic poets gazed) at the sublimity of mountain peaks; the ambrosial miracle of falling in love; the miraculous experience of what the philosopher Paul Brunton[87] called a "glimpse," the opening of a window onto another order of being. Be that as it may, it is virtually inevitable that the moment we gain an authentic glimpse of the brilliance of that divine nature, we—like Psyche in the myth—instinctively attempt to seize and own it and, in that very impulse and act, lose what we most desire. This is devastating and can literally break our heart, as it does—just about—Psyche's. You'll remember that, after Eros's departure, she tries to kill herself and is saved only by the river god and, afterward, by the god Pan's good advice. And what is Pan's counsel? Do not end yourself in despair, but go in quest of Love, and strive to find and reclaim what you feel you have lost forever. That hope, says the god of Nature, is the only cure for the emptiness lodged like an arrow in your heart of hearts.

And so, Psyche follows the old sage's counsel. After futile attempts to find shelter in the temples of other goddesses (Ceres, Hera), she finally hands herself over to the one who long ago had placed a bounty on her head: the true goddess of Beauty, the divine Aphrodite. At the behest of the goddess, Psyche embarks upon the series of tasks that comprise her long path toward what ultimately may—if she perseveres—turn into a more conscious relation to Love and to all the divine sources of her being, the sphere of the gods or archetypal powers that comprise the numinous ground of existence.

So do not be mistaken. Psyche's long road is no casual or accidental matter. It is a spiritual path, every bit as challenging as the fasting and praying, the constant chanting of mantras, or endless meditations that perhaps comprise more widely recognized images of such. At the same time, however, it *is* different, for it is her—psyche or soul's *own* path—the path true to her essential nature which (as Hillman emphasizes) inheres, first and foremost, in her innate beauty. Psyche's (the soul's) path—is thus, intrinsically and essentially, an *aesthetic* adventure, a wandering odyssey that entails her education in the means and methods of soul-making, the poetics of mind. Another "Western" culture called a kindred trail: Walking the Path of Beauty.[88]

For we must also be careful <u>not</u> to be fooled by the fairy-tale-like portrayal of Aphrodite in the story as a vain, mean, rather ungoddesslike prospective mother-in-law. She is, after all, divine Beauty, and Psyche's path is aimed and directed as much toward her as toward Eros: toward Love *and* Beauty, for the one is child of the other. And both—on account of their divine, archetypal natures—are, in the way of all gods, sublime, and, in the very radiance of their divine aura, terrible.

Near the beginning of the *Duino Elegies*, Rilke writes: "For Beauty is nothing/but the beginning of Terror/we're still just able to bear . . . because it serenely disdains to destroy us."[89] In the myth, though, Aphrodite seems *not* so serenely intent upon, in fact, destroying Psyche, who, mortal and uninitiated as she is, hardly knows her way around the divine mysteries or when and how she is overstepping her rightful bounds. (If you want a feel for this dynamic, and most everything else having to do with the myth, I cannot recommend enough C. S. Lewis's retelling of the myth in his novel *Till We Have Faces*[90]). And yet, her labors are in fact, just that: a path of initiation, progressive steps enabling her to build her imaginative capacities so as to remake her soul into a fit vessel of vision, one finally able to bear genuine, and mutually beneficial, relationship with the divine. And the character of that crucial first step, Psyche's first labor?

Let us look at it this way. As Hillman tells us in *Anima Mundi:*

> There is also Aphrodite who was called the world soul in Ficino's translation of Plotinus and to whom Ficino awards the sensate world. To grasp the Greek account of perception, psychology must already, as did Psyche in Apulieus' tale, stand in the temple of Aphrodite, recognizing that each thing smiles, has allure, calls forth *aisthesis.* "Calling forth," provoking, *kaleo:* this was Ficino's derivation of Aphrodite's main characteristic, *kallos,* beauty.[91]

And so, Aphrodite is, too, not only the celestial but also world soul, *anima mundi.* And Psyche can, initially, no more bear unreflected sight of her whole radiance than she can look straight at the sun of love without being stunned. Even so, she who stands for *kallos,* beauty . . . we see the unmistakable trace of her being in all the many things of the world, each and every one of which reflects some facet, some feature, some image of her in its own particular gemlike way. And in learning to see the smile on the face of things, to catch that image in the creative mirror of the poetic mind and so *name* it—as Rilke did, again and again, so consummately in his *New Poems*—that is indeed a great first step forward on the soul's own long path toward all that it has ever loved and thinks it may have lost forever.

Sixth Lecture

Soul Schooling

James Hillman's archetypal psychology is not a self-consistent system of philosophy, and there are many rabbit holes ready to trip up those exploring the field replanted by this fertile thinker. Perhaps the deepest of these involves the problem of the self. Hillman, in his zeal to overthrow the historic dominion of the *ego* as such derives from the Cartesian *cogito,* often seems to buy into the notion that the very concept—or archetypal idea—of *individual identity per se* is so bound up with this particular historic construction that the two cannot be effectively sundered.

And indeed, how can we mean anything essentially different from just this *ego* when we—translating Descartes into plain English—think and say "I"? Are not the idea of the ego and the first person singular irreducible equivalents, and do not both refer to one and the same thing: the self-identity of that reflexive form of thought, of intelligent consciousness, that—as Descartes so clearly recognized—seems the axiomatic ground of our very being and existence per se?

Well, yes—and no, says Hillman, putting the accent (despite the incontestable singularity and force of his own individual character) on that "no." And with good reason, for (as we have been trying to show in these lectures), when we identify our human being, the essence of our soul-nature, with just this necessary but narrow construction, we effectively cut the identity of our soul off from the world, and vice versa. Not only that, we also estrange ourselves—our souls—from God or the realm of Spirit because (as we have likewise indicated) the very idea of the self-constituting subject effectively usurps the form of self-presence—unconditioned being-in-itself—that is traditionally the prerogative of (not the human but) the divine mind. Descartes himself *may* have been a devout deist, but the logic underpinning his philosophy leads directly to both a secularized (and so atheistic) science and—correlatively—a thoroughly subject-centered ego-psychology.

Hillman, wanting none of the above and passionately desiring to reopen the soul to the world of the gods as well as to the gods at large in the world, relentlessly critiques the historic conflation of *the identity of the human soul* with the (all-too-human) ego. For the soul, argues Hillman, is so much more—and so much less—than that; so much more and so much less than we have construed it to be in the wake of Augustine, Harvey, Descartes and Kant.

We owe Hillman an inestimable debt for his brilliant campaign on behalf of the soul. His reenvisioning of psychology has given the field a new lease on life. And yet it does sometimes seem that he goes so far as to throw out the baby—the child of soul we human beings are—with the alchemical bath water; that his psychology retains no place—none of honor, at least—for any idea of self as such may be understood as (not mere egoity but) a concrete expression of the essence of soul; or, correlatively, an idea of soul as such may be understood as the gist and ground of our own distinctly human individual identity. I speak, that is to say, of any teaching of *self as soul* and vice versa.

I say "sometimes" advisedly, for several of Hillman's late books—notably, *The Soul's Code*[92] and *The Force of Character*[93]—implicitly endorse and indeed amplify such understanding. Nonetheless, the main body of his work remains, at best, theoretically ambivalent on this score. Ever on guard against any move that might lead the rebel soul to be captured and dragged in chains back to languish as a prisoner in the castle of the sovereign ego, Hillman does not really embrace the classical Jungian paradigm that revolves around the critical difference between the Self and the ego, and focuses psychological vision upon a process of individuation, a heroic journey by means of which the psyche moves toward the end of a wholeness ultimately understood as realization of the Self. Such a paradigm, one could well contend, is anathema to the dispersive and centrifugal force of Hillman's discourse.

And yet: Hillman's is, by his own admission, a psychology of soul-making. And so we may well ask: Can this central idea—the archetypal notion of soul-making itself—ultimately remain estranged from the idea of that unity of personality we customarily call "self"? More pointedly, can the very idea of soul—as such may be regarded to be the heart of the mortal human psyche—remain coherent if denied its share of that unity and continuity, that self-sameness, characteristic of the identity of any authentic being?

These may be considered metaphysical questions and Hillman, for all his theoretical brilliance, generally shies away from such. And yet such concerns, metaphysical as they may be, are by no means without practical force and challenge us to take another, closer look at the foundation stone of his archetypal psychology. What does he (or we) really mean by that pivotal concept—*soul-making*—after all?

We can pursue this question by tracing the key phrase back to its literary source. Hillman borrows the term "soul-making" from John Keats, who coined it in a letter to his siblings. George and Georgiana Keats, having recently emigrated, were living in Kentucky at the time, and it is tempting to query whether this remarkable letter's American address was purely coincidental. Keats wrote it just two years before his tragically premature death at the age of 25. It is long, rambling, and brilliant, and—given the questions we have framed—I think it will serve us well to take time to read, not just the frequently quoted phrase that Hillman himself borrowed, but the lengthy discussion in which that phrase is embedded. And so, Keats:

> The common cognomen of this world among the misguided and superstitious is 'a vale of tears' from which we are to be redeemed by a certain arbitrary interposition of God and taken to Heaven. What a little circumscribed straightened notion! Call the world if you Please "The vale of Soul-making." Then you will find out the use of the world (I am speaking now in the highest terms for human nature admitting it to be immortal which I will here take for granted for the purpose of showing a

> thought which has struck me concerning it). I say 'Soul making'—Soul as distinguished from an Intelligence. There may be intelligences or sparks of the divinity in millions-but *they are not Souls till they acquire identities, till each one is personally itself.* [emphasis added][94]

Here already, we find the motif of the *soul* and its *making* originally linked to the process of acquiring unique personal identity. Keats continues:

> I[n]telligences are atoms of perception-they know and they see and they are pure, in short they are God. How then are Souls to be made? How then are these sparks which are God to have identity given them-so as ever to possess a bliss peculiar to each one's individual existence? How, but by the medium of a world like this? This point I sincerely wish to consider because I think it a grander system of salvation than the chrystian religion-or rather it is a system of Spirit-creation. This is effected by three grand materials acting the one upon the other for a series of years. These three Materials are the *Intelligence,* the *human heart* (as distinguished from intelligence or Mind) and the *World or*

> *Elemental* space suited for the proper action of *Mind and Heart* on each other for the purpose of forming the *Soul or Intelligence destined to possess the sense of Identity.*[95]

Again, Keats conceives of Soul in conjunction with the forming of "the sense of identity." He completes his line of thought with an original and telling analogy:

> I can scarcely express what I but dimly perceive-and yet I think I perceive it-that you may judge the more clearly I will put it in the most homely form possible-I will call the *world* a School instituted for the purpose of teaching little children to read. I will call the *human heart hornbook* used in that School-and I will call the *Child able to read, the Soul* made from that *school* and its *hornbook.* Do you not see how necessary a World of Pains and troubles is to school an Intelligence and make it a Soul? A Place where the heart must feel and suffer in a thousand diverse ways! Not merely is the Heart a Hornbook, It is the Mind's Bible, it is the Mind's experience, it is the teat from which the Mind or intelligence sucks its identity—As various as the Lives of Men are—so various

> become their Souls, and thus does God make individual beings, Souls, Identical Souls of the Sparks of his own essence. This appears to me a faint sketch of a system of Salvation which does not affront our reason and humanity—I am convinced that many difficulties which Christians labour under would vanish before it.[96]

So, it turns out that—for Keats at least—soul-making is all about the forging of identity, the making of "individual beings, souls." How then is the rubric of soul-making not, after all, a disguised form of ego-psychology?

Its emphasis on individual identity notwithstanding, Keats's metaphysical framework clearly exceeds the bounds of any purely subject-centered psychology. He begins, after all, not with the Self but rather with God—although he does not conceive of deity in any personal or anthropomorphic form but instead as "intelligences or sparks of the divinity in millions." While incommensurate with our usual monotheistic God-image, this is no unprecedented notion born of a Romantic poet's eccentric fancy. It derives from the Platonic vision of "God" as *Nous* or Divine Mind, the origin of the Ideal Forms that provide the intelligible ground of creation—those Forms or logoi that constitute, at the level most proximate to manifestation, the multifaceted "Mind" or Intelligence of *anima mundi.* These "intelligences" or "sparks of divinity" (Jung, in an alchemical context, refers to them as "scintillae"[97]) may be understood as well to be, if not themselves the metaphysical origin of what Jung and Hillman call "archetypes," at least entailed or implicated in such.[98] And if such supply the ultimate (and ultimately divine) ground of the formation of individual identity, we find ourselves—even while groping toward an idea of the genesis and development of such identity—far outside the province of any narrow ego psychology.

Keats's system takes as its premise his own version of the spirit-soul-matter triad, although he reserves the term "soul" for the entity—the distinct *identity*—that emerges as a result of the creative interplay of Mind, Heart, and World. I have provided some preliminary guidance as to how we might begin to understand the nature of that Mind, but what of the central term in Keats's scheme, the Mind's Bible, "the teat from which the Mind or Intelligence sucks its identity" and in so doing makes (a) soul?

The whole mysterious process so cryptically referenced must undoubtedly count as the heart of the matter. We are speaking (to put a Jungian spin on it) of the very engine of individuation. And Keats's rather idiosyncratic terminology does provide us with a clue as to how we may understand the central, the pivotal term of the process of soul-making. This, in the parlance of our poet, is nothing other than the Heart in its mediative relation to the Mind and the World, or what we (following Hillman and Corbin) have been construing as those processes (simultaneously and inseparably *imaginative, aesthetic, and poetic*) that comprise *the thought of the heart.*

So it is that when James Hillman, in his seminal opus, revisions psychology as a system of soul-making and names the four chief modes of such, he is in fact elaborating primary (archetypal, if you will) forms of poetic imagination. The integral cooperation of these chief modes accomplishes, as one most noteworthy *effect*, the formation of individual identity, the forging of the *self* as *soul* and *soul* as that authentically existent being-in-the-world we could refer to (as does Emerson in the title of his famous essay[99]) as "self."

Even so, this most certainly does NOT entail refunding the riddle of the Sphinx—the mystery of who and what we are and, too, how we come to be so—to the Cartesian or the heroically Oedipal ego; the self narrowly identified with (and generated by) rational-cognitive-problem-solving consciousnesses. *On the contrary,* it reveals the self as soul (and soul as self) to be the *supplementary effect* of methods of soul-making that can in no wise be compassed by egocentric cognitive processes. Those methods are, irreducibly and in essence, modes of *creative imagination* that can only be properly explored under the aegis of—no analytic logic—but the poetics of Mind. We are concerned here with the paths by which Keats's "divine sparks"—those archetypal intelligences or ideas—connect *to* and interact *with* the body of the world by way of the transformative activity of the Mind's Bible, that sacred Hornbook. To explore such paths is to probe mysteries that can be approached only by virtue of that same organ that performs the miracle of creation, the same effective agency: the poetic inspiration of the thought of the heart.

Nor should we, at the present juncture, find ourselves at a loss with respect to means and methods of this same exploration, for we have already in fact begun to avail ourselves of such. Hillman's exegesis of the four modes of soul-making in *Revisioning* provides critical orientation for such inquiry, but he himself as much as admits that in and of itself his theoretical discourse cannot fully engage the heart of the matter. More pregnant (especially when read in conjunction with *Revisioning*) is that imaginal template that Hillman himself endorses as the *mythic* ground of his soul-making psychology. For make no mistake: The path of soul-making—and so, in Keats's system, the road toward realization of individual identity—is nothing other than the path that Psyche treads in her pursuit of Eros; the long and winding road of her labors of love.

To digest the import of this imaginal truth is to understand, at a deeper level, the true force of Hillman's critique of any psychology of selfhood—including Jung's own. Because if, reflecting upon the Pysche-Eros story, we focus our attention upon the marrow of the myth—namely, Psyche's tasks—we realize that the idea of selfhood plays little or no role here; does not figure in at either the beginning or the end of her path. On the contrary, Psyche starts her laborious journey in a state of hopeless self-negation (she is saved from suicide only by the good offices of the river god and the counsel of Pan); and her end—the *goal* of her quest—never has anything to do with any notion of self-realization, psychic wholeness, or the like. That end, from first to last—is *reunion with Love*— which aim coincides with that of becoming lawfully related to divine Beauty (her prospective mother-in-law, Aphrodite). In fact, it would be fair to say that Psyche, for the most part, couldn't care less about her *self as such:* in her own eyes, her life is nigh worthless, without value or purpose or meaning *except* insofar she may live in hope of regaining Love; reclaiming, that is, her original connection with the divine being whose terrible beauty led her—in that sublime yet awful moment when she lights the lamp of consciousness—to open her sleeping eyes.

Still, we must be clear: None of this means that—from start to finish and all along the way—Psyche is not in fact herself, that there is not an essential continuity of being subsisting between the beautiful young girl we encounter at the beginning of the story and the bride of Eros welcomed into the circle of Gods at the end. This is true even if we need, as well, acknowledge the complementary truth: namely, that the initiate Psyche fit to drink the ambrosia of the Gods is hardly the same creature as the innocent daughter of the king. The two are as like, and unlike, as the earthbound caterpillar and the airy butterfly aloft and soaring on gorgeous wings.

And what is, after all, most material to us, as seekers, is not any theoretical argument as to whether these are or are not the self-same being, but the nature and dynamic of the intervening changes, the transfiguring character of the stages in-between.

And these (so our argument runs) are *imaginative* changes, types of transformation *theoretically* articulated as Hillman's modes of soul-making, *mythically* symbolized by Psyche's four labors, and *poetically enacted* in the itinerary of Rilke's literary opus, the progression of his life-work from the *New Poems* to

Malte to the *Elegies* and, finally, the culmination of his prophetic oeuvre, *Sonnets to Orpheus.*

In the last lecture, we discussed the personifying poetics characteristic of Rilke's *New Poems*. Chapter 10 of *In the Image of Orpheus* links both to Psyche's first labor. Now, as it happens, the Rilke text we are devoted to this week entertains a special relationship to the heart and soul of Keats's remarkable musings. "Call the world if you Please 'The vale of Soul-making'" Keats declares, later adding: "Do you not see how necessary a World of Pains and troubles is to school an Intelligence and make it a Soul? A Place where the heart must feel and suffer in a thousand diverse ways!" A world of pains and troubles . . . a heart that feels and suffers in a thousand ways. . . One could hardly come up with a more fitting gloss of Rilke's *Malte,* better headlines for the (non-)story told in his (anti-)heroic odyssey.

I say *non-* and *anti-* because while, generically speaking, the *novel* is often considered the modern stand-in for the ancient epic, Rilke's *Malte* offers nothing like a classic storyline of audacious action and daunting obstacles bravely overcome. Indeed, *The Notebooks*, composed as a collage of often disparate journal entries, hardly gives us any plot at all, any unfolding of events as such might accord with a coherent causal logic anchored in the protagonist's character. More often than not,

Malte's journal entries bear witness, not to heroic deeds expressive of conscious resolve, but to his incipient fear-driven mental illness. We encounter no self-possessed ego advancing by virtue of incisive intellect and deliberate will but instead are made party to a (largely unconscious) process of . . . *falling apart.* What is going on here; what type of imaginative activity does Malte so (un)dramatically display?

Let us address this question by way of two distinct yet related chief points.

First, let's lean on Hillman. What Malte is doing so much of the time is exactly what Hillman so aptly calls *pathologizing*, the second mode of soul-making introduced and amplified in *Revisioning.* The first chapter on *Malte* in the *Soul History* discusses this nigredo-related form of imaginative transformation at length. Here I would like to add a further perspective that highlights the connection between *Malte,* the triadic nucleus of Keats's "system of salvation," and the main theme of last week's lecture, the ensouled character of the world.

The *Soul History* makes the point that while Rilke's *New Poems* chiefly explores the world of things as such present themselves in external (or outer) space, *Malte* investigates the more interior and subjective domain of *personal history* as this extends in and through imaginal time. ("I have an inner self of which I was ignorant. Everything goes thither now"[100] writes Malte.) This difference is patent and significant, and yet should not be construed too categorically. On the one hand, on account of Rilke's personifying, *all* the objects in *New Poems* possess an inner dimension and subjective depth. On the other, the intensely inward dimension of Malte's multifaceted musings notwithstanding, his imagination unfolds in concert with his experience of that "Vale of soul-making" we call the World. The famous first sentence of the novel ("So then one does come here in order to live; I would have sooner thought one died here"[101]) places Malte's psychology in the context of his urban environment. The whole first entry (one which sets the tone for the whole book) records Malte's aesthetic (olfactory, tactile, kinesthetic and—always—mood- and value-charged) responses to the varied features of his surroundings, and so makes palpably evident that Malte's Parisian world reflects his state of mind—*and* vice versa.

And Malte's *is* a pathologized eye, one that habitually focuses upon the blurring of boundaries that results from decay, disintegration and death, all of which processes involve the transition of things from one state to another; even the passing of things (including, Malte fears, himself) from being to nonbeing. Such reality can be dim, grim, depressing—indeed maddeningly so. At the same time, it is the ground of change, transformation and (potentially) renewal.

This brings us to the second chief point. To articulate it, we may rely again on Hillmanian theory and, too, the Psyche-Eros story. Hillman, as you know, proposes a radical change in the mythic matrix that nourishes psychological vision; advocates replacing therapeutic means and methods that derive from the Oedipus narrative with alternative measures suggested by the Psyche-Eros tale. The *Soul History* elaborates how Rilke's *Malte* effectively models just this critical purpose by virtue of its poetic enactment of chief features of this major (lifesaving?) operation of myth-replacement. We have here, in our brief discussion of *Malte's* anti-heroic plotlessness, already alluded to crucial elements of this transformative rewriting, but I want to conclude this lecture by amplifying still another motif mentioned but incompletely interpreted in the *Soul History*.

The famous Cluny[102] tapestry sequence *The Lady and the Unicorn* plays a pivotal role in *The Notebooks of Malte Laurids Brigge*. This is true not only formally (Malte's lengthy dialogue with the tapestries take place in the middle of the text) but thematically as well. This is so, I would suggest, in part because the archetypal imagery of the tapestry both emerges from and reveals the deep underlying connection between *Malte* and the Psyche-Eros mythologem.

What passes for "action" in *Malte* is, generally speaking, anima-driven. The latter half of the text in particular features numerous feminine figures: Malte's mother, his cousin Abelone (Malte's first love and the person to whom he, in a kind of active imagination, shows the tapestries); the long litany of great woman lovers; the poet Sappho. The prose evoking and amplifying these figures makes clear that *The Notebooks* ultimately revolves around—no worldly conflict—but the soul's quest for Love. That quest (Christine de Pisan's "way of long learning") inevitably involves "a world of pain and troubles," a place "where the heart feels and suffers," for only so may Psyche learn the purificatory lessons that qualify her to become the bride of Eros. A kindred mythological motif (one closely related, in particular, to the symbolism of Psyche's *second* labor) announces itself, silently but powerfully, in the archetypal imagery of *The Lady and the Unicorn.*

We may first of all remark that, insofar as it is the Lady herself that is the centerpiece of all the tapestries, the entire sequence clearly revolves around the soul in its feminine aspect, the soul qua anima, Psyche with a capital "P." The whole series has most often been interpreted as representing portrayals of the five senses. Gottfried Büttner,[103] however, flatly rejects this questionable interpretation (after all, there are six, not five tapestries), suggesting instead the more satisfying idea that the tapestries represent various stages in the maturation of the soul, phases of its progress toward a spiritual goal. Unfortunately, we do not have time here to interpret the sequence in this manner, but the key to the whole lies in the relationship between the Lady and the heraldic animals that flank her: the Lion and (especially) the Unicorn. And with respect to this question, Jung and his knowledge of alchemy can offer material aid.

In fact, Jung devotes the last chapter of *Psychology and Alchemy* ("Alchemical Symbolism in the History of Religion") to "The Paradigm of the Unicorn." Earlier in the same book, Jung identifies Mercurius (as well as Christ and the Lapis stone) as a symbol of the Self. In this last chapter, he states unequivocally: "Lion and unicorn are both symbols of Mercurius."[104] Refining this equation, Jung continues to associate the Unicorn with "Mercurius . . . in his volatile form of *spiritus.*"[105] Interpreting another, different lady and unicorn image, he states: "The virgin represents (Mercurius's) passive, feminine aspect, while the unicorn or the lion illustrates the wild, rampant, masculine penetrating force of the *spiritus mercurialis.*"[106]

Well and good, but how does this aid our understanding of the underlying connection between *Malte* and the Psyche-Eros mythologem?

When Jung, in reference to the Lion and Unicorn, speaks of a "wild, rampant, masculine penetrating force," his language readily calls up the image of the tempestuous golden rams (themselves horned creatures) of Psyche's second labor. The labor itself may be construed to contain a twofold lesson. Psyche needs to learn the lesson of rhythm and of patience; understand that, while solar power may be killing when faced at full force at midday, that seminal spiritual energy can be safely and creatively engaged at the twilit hour of dusk when light and dark, yin and yang are naturally in balance. Soul cannot seize the energy of spirit directly or immediately but rather by way of a deferred response that involves a more gradual and painstaking process: namely, the deliberate gathering of the golden wool from twigs and branches long after the rams themselves are gone.

That gathering may be understood to be symbolic of a process of *memory*, a *recollection* of the fiery power of spirit, the divine light of consciousness that cannot be faced or seen directly but the golden threads of which can and indeed must be *remembered.* This anima-driven soul-making endeavor cannot, moreover, be construed as an activity of ego-consciousness but rather goes forward under the auspices of what Hillman, in the *Myth of Analysis,* calls *not* by the negative designation of "the unconscious" but (in accord with a time-worn but neglected tradition): *memoria.*[107]

And what does one do with strands of wool? Weave them together to make textile, and perhaps—eventually—a tapestry, or a series of tapestries the interwoven images of which tell a kind of story, albeit one that does not necessarily display an obvious plot.

It is just such a soul-making process of *recollection*; just such a process of regathering and imaginatively weaving together strands of memory, that Rilke gives us in *The Notebooks of Malte Laurids Brigge.* The novel itself is, after all, a poetic textile; even, one could say, a kind of tapestry. Rilke himself called it a mosaic, which kindred term means, literally, "patient work worthy of the muses." That is, I think, a most fitting moniker for the gold wool-gathering work of Psyche's second labor.

The invocation of the muse implies too that this weaving is a kind of creative storytelling, even a myth-making, and all traditional cultures recognize such as the chief means of looking into the question of the human self, construing who and what we are. In *The Notebooks of Malte Laurids Brigge* we find Rilke hard at work reinventing his personal history, producing what

Hillman calls "healing fiction."[108] In the letter to Lou in which he explains his reasons for not entering formal analysis,[109] Rilke explicitly calls his poetic work a form of self-treatment. In *Malte*, he is about the therapeutic business of reimagining what he called his "other self" so that the mirror of his own soul—cleared of fear—might finally catch, in its reflective surface, an image of that elusive spirit so indispensable to the forging of individual identity, that holy spirit which Rilke and Jung and the Lady (aka, Soul or Psyche) know in the guise of some mythical creature—a Unicorn, or the fiery mercurial penetrating character of (the god of) Love.

Seventh Lecture

"Who, if I Cried" – The Prophetic Strain

Wer, wenn ich schriee, hörte mich denn aus der Engel / Ordnungen? und gesetzt selbst, as nähme einer mich plötzlich ans Herz: ich verginge von seinem / stärkeren Dasein. Denn das Schöne ist nichts als des Schrecklichen Anfang . . .

Who, if I cried, would hear me among the angelic / orders? And even if one of them suddenly pressed me against his heart, I should fade in the strength of his / stronger existence. For Beauty's nothing but the beginning of Terror . . .[110]

The *Duino Elegies* begin with heart-rending lament, a cry of existential despair. The estrangement from the divine it sounds so powerfully and so poignantly, although uttered in a foreign tongue, rings familiar, for the language of pain is universal. What sensitive soul has not felt similar desolation? A kindred sense that, whatever prayer she may send forth into the cosmos, she will hear in response nothing but the faded echo of her own yearning? And if audible to souls across the span of time, Rilke's cry rings peculiarly true to us, for his may well be heard as one of the signature voices of modernity.

Yet to recognize that voice is not the same as to understand it. That requires an ear for the past that is never really . . . past, an attunement to history that leads us, too, toward a more human future.

And so it is that, in these lectures, we have recurrently referred to certain fundamental parameters of being called *spirit, soul,* and *matter* or *worldly existence* and addressed ourselves to the *relations between* and *permutations of* the terms of this triad as such characterize one or another historic development. We have spoken of the heart of Harvey and the Cartesian splitting of spirit and matter that elides soul, and how this dualism transforms into opposing monisms (the religion of the church on one side and that of science on the other). We have evoked a still earlier, less ossified separation of spirit and matter and, too, the original emergence of the soul as an independent form of individual consciousness in-between, a development associated with the advent of lyric poetry in Ancient Greece. We have touched upon psychology's own complicity in metaphysical dualism in its privileging of the human subject vis-a-vis a supposedly inanimate world. We have addressed the manner in which Rilke—from his early work through his *New Poems* and *Malte*—worked to transform the polarized universe he inherited, strove to reclaim a place for the soul in-between spiritual and material realms in such a way that the continuity between these might be regained and the cleft heart of humanity healed.

Against this background, and in the context of the hope for such healing that Rilke's work seems to hold out, we may—despite the progressive darkening of his poetic palette after his departure from Worpswede—be somewhat taken aback by the opening of Rilke's *Duino Elegies*. For the *Elegies*, after all, are not just any New Poem; nor are they the jumbled *Notebooks* of the sensitive but troubled character Rilke could call his "other self" and from whom he could distance himself when readers identified him too closely with that literary persona. The voice that speaks the *Elegies* is—unlike Malte's—indubitably the poet's own. From the moment of the poem's dramatic conception on the balcony of Duino Castle high above the Adriatic Sea, Rilke regarded the (still unfinished) cycle as his masterwork-to-be, his *magnum opus*, the definitive statement of his poetic religion. And so, from the first, although he had written only one or two, Rilke knew that, if he indeed accomplished his high mission, there were to be exactly *ten Elegies;* no more and no less. *Ten:* one and zero, being and nonbeing, rubbing shoulders; *ten*—one, two, three, and four stacked and added on top of each other and so an esoteric number of completion; *ten,* the number of the Commandments passed from God to Moses, the prophet and lawgiver who founded the tradition that has, for millennia, defined "religion" in the Western world.

And so we may be forgiven if we find ourselves startled and even dismayed at, not only the despairing tone but the message of those opening lines. For the lines speak with ruthless honesty *not* of the healing of the divide between spirit and matter, divine agency and mortal consciousness, but, on the contrary, still and yet again of the unbridgeable gulf between these, the chasm cutting our own human being-in-the-world off from the numinous realm of the sacred, from the hearing of God and his divine ambassador, the sublime yet overpowering Angel.

Rilke maintained that his Angel was Islamic rather than Christian in character. Be that as it may (and the *Soul History* has a fair bit to say on the subject), the topos of the poem is undoubtedly biblical. It is no accident that, before conceiving the *Elegies,* Rilke was reading (nay—devouring) religious sources: the Bible (above all, *Genesis,* the biblical myth of Creation), the Lives of the Saints, and—for the first time, and avidly—the Quran. This clues us into the truth that in the *Elegies,* Rilke is digging once more (as he did in his *Christ Visions* and in his *Book of Hours*) at our religious roots, drawing from the source of the spiritual stream that has, for centuries, shaped and determined the dominant image of God in the West. And he does so, once more and yet ever more consciously, as neither a *believer* nor an *unbeliever*, for such an opposition remains entrenched in the terrain circumscribed by doctrine, and the poet's mind and heart (we can say again, the *thought* of his *heart*) knows no such bounds. The poet Rilke read the Bible and the Quran not to absorb theology or codes of moral law but to empower him to speak with a voice of kindred power and authority, to inspire and to strengthen him in his own prophetic calling, the high mission of giving voice to the Word as it will and must be spoken, not at the foot of Sinai three millennia ago, or Jerusalem's temple steps 2,000 some-odd years before his—before our—time; but far more urgently *here* and *now*, on the threshing floor of modernity, that *dürftiger Zeit* (needy time) when the God—or gods—that were, are no more, and the God—or gods—to come are yet to be, are yet to reveal themselves so as to shake the earth beneath our feet and thunder admonition at the senseless brutality that, more and more, masquerades as humanity on the face of the globe.

The biblical tenor of the Elegies resounds powerfully in its very first line, a line that echoes Psalm 130, the famous *De profundis*. It does so, moreover, in a manner that—even as it strikes this biblical chord—does so in a different, more dissonant key, one that sets in stark relief the dramatic contrast between our modern poet-prophet's spiritual situation and that of his ancient forebearer.

> Who, if I cried out, would hear me among the angelic
> orders?

Thus, the voice of the Elegies. The King James version of the Psalm opens:

> Out of the depths have I cried unto thee, O
> LORD.
> LORD, hear my voice: let thine ears be attentive
> to the voice of my supplication.[111]

Elsewhere, I have written:

> Both Elegy and Psalm commence with an "I" who cries out—*or consciously decides not to*; and a (putative) addressee, who is—*or is not*—

> presumed capable of hearing. Strikingly, the Elegy's *renunciation* of the call or cry marks a rift, a seemingly unbridgeable gulf, between the human and the divine . . . a predicament wholly incommensurate with the confident and trusting tone that ultimately prevails in the Psalm.[112]

Not only do the first words of the *Elegies* dramatically contrast those of the Psalm, they clash still more spectacularly with both the tenor and the message of Rilke's *Book of Hours.* In that early prayer book, Rilke imagines himself to be thoroughly intimate with a God who is no alien terror or beauty but a close neighbor, and indeed one often dependent on the care and attention of the poet:

> You, Neighbor God, when sometimes I wake you
> with loud knocks in the night,
> it is because I seldom hear you breathe
> and know: you are alone in the room.
>
> And when you need something, there is no one
> to put the drink into your hand.
> I am always listening. Send a little sign.
> I am very near.

> Only a thin wall stands, by chance, between us;
> any moment, a cry from your mouth
> or from mine—
> and it will fall without a sound.[113]

Here we find the same theme as in the opening of the *Elegies*: the distance (or lack thereof) between human and divine being, and the possibility of communication—speech and effective hearing—between them. But with respect to how matters stand in this connection, the two poems present diametrically opposed scenarios. In the *Book of Hours,* it is the poet who portrays himself as the auditor, who is indeed "always listening," and God's cry (or the poet's own) can, at any moment, break down the inconsequential barrier (I cannot help thinking of adjacent rooms in cheap hotels) separating the poet and his God. In the Elegy, on the other hand, not only is it the poet who is the one in need—dire, spiritual need—but he harbors no illusion that the divine Angel may hear the lament of his too-human voice. And if the Angel *were* to do so, and to answer, the incommensurability of divine and human being is, in any event, so great that it would virtually destroy the poet.

And here, remember, we are not even speaking of God but merely (!) of his angelic messenger. As far as God himself is concerned, later, in this First Elegy, the poet admits to himself: "Not that you could endure / the voice of God—far from it."[114] So in the *Elegies,* the incommensurability, the difference in kind and in power, is so huge that direct contact of any sort, any effective speaking and hearing, does not even come into question.

How then do we account for this critical difference internal to Rilke's own life and work? How do we comprehend <u>both</u> the *Book of Monastic Life* <u>and</u> the *Duino Elegies* as works integral to a coherent Rilkean vision, the worldview elaborated in his poetic opus?

Of course, one could argue, we cannot. One could claim that the patent difference between the two works cannot truly be bridged, that each may stand as an authentic expression of Rilke's spirit, but do so at such diverse junctures that no path connecting the two, and so revealing an underlying unity, can fairly be traced.

This might well be considered a plausible—indeed, on the face of the poetic evidence, very credible—position. And yet, if we were to assume it, we would contradict the poet's own deeply considered stance on the matter. For in the well-known letter to the Polish translator of the *Elegies,* written just a year before his death, Rilke makes clear that he conceives his poetic oeuvre to be all of a piece, an organic development forming a consistent whole:

> I regard [the *Duino Elegies*] as a further elaboration of those essential premises that were already given in the *Book of Hours,* that in the two parts of the *New Poems* tentatively played with the image of the world and that then in *Malte,* contracted in conflict, strike back into life and there almost lead to the proof that this life so suspended in the bottomless is impossible. In the *Elegies,* starting from the same postulates, life becomes possible again, indeed it experiences here that ultimate affirmation to which young Malte, though on the difficult right path "des longues études," was as yet unable to conduct it . . . . I am amazed that the *Sonnets to Orpheus* . . . filled with the same essence, are not more helpful to you in the understanding of the *Elegies.*[115]

In accord with Rilke's statement, what we are in fact dealing with here (in relation to *The Book of Hours* and the *Elegies*) are not two fundamentally foreign inspirations but rather two quite distinct yet interrelated moments in the unfolding of Rilke's imaginative life, two discrete stations of one individual history, two different chapters in the saga of the making of the poet's soul, the forging of his mature identity. To better understand them as such, we may simply continue the principal thread of this lecture, these ruminations that aim to place Rilke's *Elegies* against the backdrop of the religious tradition the poem reinscribes and reforms.

The Judeo-Christian tradition takes its point of departure from belief in an all-powerful God whose principal home is—not Earth—but elsewhere, in that transcendent realm called Heaven or in a realm that lies even above and beyond that firmament. This God, moreover, is radically *other* than the human beings who worship—or fail—to worship him. The difference between the almighty and perfect God and mortal humankind, between the timeless realm of Heaven and the temporal sphere of Earth, thus functions as the original and constitutive premise of the tradition. At the same time, the whole point of the religion inheres in the possibility of overcoming, in whole or in part, this original division. Such is the all-important work of *redemption.*

The redeemed state, and the means to it, finds various figurations in the tradition. Christianity imagines redemption to come by way of salvation of the human soul in and through the Christ who is both God and Man, and so bridges the difference. Popular strains of the faith often do not emphasize redemption of the Earth itself, focusing upon the ascent of the saved soul to the abode of the Father in Heaven, as imagined in Rilke's own first *Vision of Christ* and dismissively cited in Keat's soulful letter:

> The common cognomen of this world among the misguided and superstitious is 'a vale of tears' from which we are to be redeemed by a certain arbitrary interposition of God and taken to Heaven. What a little circumscribed straightened notion![116]

Deeper strains of Christianity understand the work of redemption to include the dissolving of the radical division between Earth and Heaven and so the salvation of—not only the Soul—but the whole creation.

Jewish imaginations of redemption, while including a strong messianic dimension, naturally do not pivot around the figure of the Christ and his mediation. Judaism's historical focus on the covenant between God and his chosen people, the nation of Israel, generates different images of the "redeemed" state. Most popularly prominent of these may be the communion of God and Israel upon the people's entrance into the Promised Land, an Edenic place like to Heaven on Earth. The great Jewish patriarchs and prophets—Moses among them—aim to shepherd the nation of Israel toward that ultimate end by way of unwavering obedience to God's Law, a Law published and made known through the Word of the prophets, who thus function as the earthly organs and messengers of divine will. A good deal of the Hebrew Bible deals with the manifold attempts of the patriarchs and prophets to keep an often recalcitrant people in strict obedience to the Law in fulfillment with the Covenant and the promised reunion.

There are, however, strands of the Old Testament that focus less exclusively upon the epic dimension of Jewish history and eschatology and enact a more intimate and heart-felt relation between the voice of the scribe and God; books that possess a powerfully *lyric* dimension. Foremost among these are the Psalms, the songs of David. The Psalms—probably composed over a period of 500 years or more beginning around the time of David's reign at the onset of the first millennium B.C.E.—may not exhibit the same kind of personal or individual consciousness Snell associates with the first ancient Greek lyrics. The historic and spiritual background of these compositions are very different, and the psalmist generally presents himself as the voice of the people of Israel rather than a private individual. Even so, the Psalms are manifestly soulful songs, incantations expressive of human longing for connection with the divine, for connection with and redemption through God.

As such, they strike a tone of intimacy, of direct address and silent dialogue, more like that found in Rilke's *Book of Hours* than anything in the New Testament.

Still, for all the poetic resonance that sounds between Rilke's own early book of prayers and the Psalms, outstanding differences are readily evident. The Psalms not only consistently express faith in the presence and beneficence of God but additionally give voice to the religious conviction that the work of redemption is firmly in his hands; that it is God, and God alone, in his infinite power and goodness, that can and will redeem not so much the psalmist himself (although the singer is clearly included in the package) as the people to whom he gives voice. This is well-illustrated in Psalm 130, and, as it is not over-long, we would do well to listen to it in its entirety to gain a better sense of the religious world from which it emerges and to which it gives concise and moving expression:

> Out of the depths have I cried unto thee, O LORD.
> Lord hear my voice: let thine ears be attentive
> to the voice of my supplications.
> If thou, LORD, shouldest mark iniquities,
> O Lord, who shall stand?
> But there is forgiveness with thee, that thou
> mayest be feared.

> I wait for the LORD, my soul doth wait,
> and in his word do I hope.
> My soul waiteth for the Lord more than they that watch for the morning: I say, more than they that watch for the morning.
> Let Israel hope in the LORD: for with the LORD there is mercy, and with him is plenteous redemption.
> And he shall redeem Israel from all his iniquities.[117]

Thus, the *De profundis*. But our modern singer's spiritual situation is markedly different. Even in the *Book of Hours*, in which Rilke—through the mouth of his monk—expresses a kindred intimacy with God, that proximity comes at the cost of God's omnipotence. It is clear right from the first poem in *The Book of Monastic Life*—one that celebrates the poet's own creative power and omits God entirely—that Rilke's chief subject is *not* going to be the traditional Almighty; that, at the very least, Rilke's God is going to share effective agency with the poet himself.

Given the historic change of scene, that is, after all, not surprising. After the erosion of traditional religion culminated in Nietzsche's proclamation of the death of God, cultured souls could hardly get around the very real question as to whether this God—indeed, any semblance of Him—could intelligently be considered to exist at all. Rilke, tutored by Lou, audaciously maintained that He was, after all, not only alive but well. And yet, this extended tenure could only be granted in conjunction with the acceptance of a radically altered relationship between divine and human being, between God and the soul who might (among other things) sing his praises. For in the wake of the long historic evolution it had undergone since its emergence in ancient Greece, the individual human soul or *psyche* had attained to a different niveau of spiritual independence vis-a-vis divine agency. No longer could she ascribe to the childlike belief that she needed only to be good and obey the Law handed down by the Fathers, and that God would take care of the rest, *including* the world-important work of redemption—whatever *that* might be taken to mean in these latter days.

And yet, that autonomy—for the most part taken for granted, and indeed tragically so today—does not come without its own spiritual as well as material price, namely, distance and detachment from the divine. In order to develop its own spiritual identity and power, the soul must naturally be cast out of Paradise, lose the privilege of a more unconscious yet more trusting proximity to God. We find one illustration of this crucial dynamic in the thoroughly unbiblical, yet nonetheless deeply relevant, mythic substructure of Rilke's own soul history, the tale of Psyche and Eros.

Before the lighting of her lamp, Psyche enjoys constant intercourse with Eros, the god of Love, under the cover of darkness—a mental as well as physical darkness that hides his divine identity from her. In fact, before the fateful revelation, Psyche suspects, but does not know for sure, that her lover is in fact a god. Her sisters—who represent less developed aspects of her own being—all but convince her that her lover is no god but, on the contrary, a powerful monster. And before lighting her lamp, before seeking to find out by the light of her own conscious mind *who* or *what* he is, Psyche herself is more or less powerless to tell the difference.

Of course, once she has seen Eros with her own awakened eyes, all doubt is put to rest. Even so, the happiness afforded by the discovery is fleeting, for the moment that she sees and seizes upon her lover's divine beauty more or less coincides with the moment that he is, inevitably, lost to her; the moment of his searing chastisement of her betrayal and his wounded departure.

Now the strange and terrible thing is this: Psyche's new certainty as to the divine pedigree of the god she loves does not initially bring her tangibly closer to him; on the contrary. She no longer has any doubt in his divinity—that doubt, like the very life of her diabolical sisters, has been forever dashed—and yet her more awakened knowledge of him is, at first, cause for nothing but heartrending loss, grief, and hopeless desolation. For it is now, and only now, that the soul becomes conscious of and so *feels* the seemingly unbridgeable distance between herself and her divine Love; now, only now, that her heart feels the killing force of the dramatic separation that results from their difference in—not *degree*—but *kind* of being. He is, after all, a god; and she—merely mortal.

And that force is indeed potentially killing. Upon her god's departure, Psyche's first impulse is to end her life. Eros's wounded flight not only deprives her of divine love; once she has seen—and lost—Him, the world itself, and her own being in it, seems utterly empty. Where there is no Love, there is no Life; where there is no possibility of relation to the divine, no authentic human being.

And so the soul finds itself, at this juncture, in a very precarious liminal state. The soul feels itself dead to the world, and the world is dead to it, and yet—at the same time—the soul feels almost hopelessly estranged from Spirit, from the very source of Love and the Reason for Being. Separated from both the realm of Spirit *and* from the Body of the World, the soul thus finds itself in that no-man's land we have, in these talks, evoked any number of times before: that emptiness at the center of Charles Wright's explicitly dualistic poem; that yawning chasm

James Hollis—by way of Jung—so aptly conjures as the ground-tone of modernity:

> When moderns fell off the roof of the medieval cathedral, Jung wrote, they fell into the abyss of the Self . . . The problem of identity and the task of cosmic location, or spiritual grounding, becomes an individual dilemma.[118]

And—need I say it?—this desolate neither-here-nor-there spiritual state is also the point of departure for Rilke's *Duino Elegies,* that great poem cycle that could only strive to heal the wound of the modern self by diving deep into the heart of the problem of identity, by proclaiming, in its very first line, the dilemma that is, at one and the same time (as our modern poet-psalmist sings) an *individual* and *world-historical* dilemma. And here, now, the solution to the problem lies, first and foremost, not in a nation's, a chosen people's, covenant with God, but in the precincts of the individual soul or mind itself, the human psyche and its—her—privileged relation to the Spirit that visits her in the form of the God of Love.

And so the key, the crucial word in the second sentence of that last paragraph is, in fact, *"almost"* . . . "*almost* hopelessly estranged from spirit." In the context of the myth, as the God Pan makes known, there does remain some hope that Psyche may find Love again—although most certainly not by way of any shortcut to the beyond, any self-drowning or leaping off a cliff or high tower. Rather she must, putting herself in the service of the dread Goddess of Beauty, embark (as Rilke said Malte did) on "the path of long learning," the fearful odyssey of her labors, her "road of trials."[119] In so doing, she may, step by poetic step, task by psychological task, educate and purify her soul and—by way of the joint effect of all these methods of soul-making—transform herself into a mortal vessel at long last worthy of divine love: that mature psyche who might unite with divine eros in the *hieros gamos* or sacred marriage.

And what, ultimately, is achieved by this other than (as if it were not enough) the soul's realization of its being in bliss (symbolized in the myth by the birth of Pleasure)? What, after all, of the World and its people?

The *Elegies* represent spiritual climax a little differently than does Apuleius and in a manner that is perhaps both less and more fulfilling than in the fable. The whole grand sweeping cycle of Ten Elegies do indeed conclude and celebrate a rather spectacular reconciliation, a reconnection between divine spirit and human soul. In the beginning, the poet of the *Elegies* laments that—if he were to cry out—no Angel would even hear him, so distantly removed is his form of human consciousness from that divine Other. The opening of the Tenth and last Elegy finds the poet singing, in triumph and jubilation, to a chorus of angels who not only hear him but assent to his joyful song. Reconciliation, reconnection indeed; but divine marriage—no.

In the *Elegies*, unlike the Psyche-Eros story, the poet's soul is not exactly lifted up into the realm of the gods but remains indefinitely and resolutely below, a denizen of the Earth. This does not, however, mean that it remains unaffected or untransformed by its spiritual reconnection; on the contrary. By virtue of the initiation undergone in and through the text (and I defer to the *Soul History's* four Elegy chapters for the relevant amplification here), the poet's soul is empowered, not to become a god, but to become, in wonderful partnership with the angelic host—a bearer of the divine Word. And that means, too, an agent of revelation—and redemption.

If this amounts, too, to a realization of what Carl Jung calls the Self, and that mature individual identity Keats calls, simply, a made soul, it is so in a manner that is, paradoxically, not in the least self-interested. Because the end of this attainment, the purpose of becoming such a *psyche-logos,* speaker of soul, or what philosopher Paul Brunton calls an organ of the interior word,[120] is not only or even primarily "self-realization." It is also transformative liberation of the (things of the) World, of earthly matters and indeed of the Earth itself. That transformation is achieved by fulfilling the destiny of the soul—our peculiarly human destiny—which consists in revelation of the true nature of things themselves, their right naming, which redemptive act discloses the World itself as a showing forth of Beauty, a theophany of spirit. And that is one modern poet-prophet's version of the traditional mission of religious redemption, the realization of a new Heaven and a new Earth.

And where is the place of this wonderful consummation? In the space of the soul itself which, as Heraclitus and Snell remind us, has its own dimension, a depth that—while infinite—is not extended in physical space. That depth—which nonetheless contains, in transfigured form, all that unredeemed vision might regard as "outer"—Rilke calls: *Weltinnenraum.*[121]

As we shall see in our next and final lecture, it is the place wherein the Tree of Life is planted.

Eighth Lecture

Rilke's Mythos – Listening In

Da stieg ein Baum. O reine Übersteigung!
O Orpheus singt! O hoher Baum im Ohr!
Und alles schwieg. Doch selbst in der Verschweigung
ging neuer Anfang, Wink und Wandlung vor.

A tree rose up. O pure transcendence!
O Orpheus sings! O tall tree in the ear!
And everything hushed. Yet in that quiet cadence
new transformations were beginning to appear.[122]

And so, in the beginning . . . or rather, *before* the beginning, before that "new beginning" ("neuer Anfang") emerging from a peculiarly pregnant *silence* ushered in (O, forest of paradox!) by song . . . And so, in the beginning, before all else—the spontaneous arising of a Tree.

But what Tree is this, and *where* does it suddenly manifest? In the *ear?* What a strange and rich figure!

One that magically transports us into . . . what enchanted world? What place is this where wild animals—accustomed to cacophonous shriek and growl—are drawn like bees to the honeyed source of sound around which they gather in rapt attention as if listening in to the secret of their own being?

To be sure, this is no ordinary world. No world (like the "interpreted world" of the First Elegy) bound and determined by our usual habits of perception. In fact, no manifestly human voice sounds here; none that (again, as in the *Elegies*) laments or celebrates the human condition. There is, it is true, a kind of joy expressed; a note, even, of exultation. But is this joy . . . *ours?* Indeed, are we (whoever we are) invited into the scene at all? Our human selves or souls drawn like the animals to the hearth of song, the music of the lyre, and sound of the poet's voice? Or do we find ourselves irremovably outside the magic circle, eavesdropping on goings-on that are not only strange but alien to us?

The answer to this question may well depend upon who we are, or (more accurately) what we have—or have not—made of ourselves. It may depend, that is, on the responsiveness of our soul, our capacity to listen and so to *hear*. For if we have developed no ear for poetry or music, for Orphic song, we may not be able to enter the temple of hearing, that place of reverence and wonder deep within the innermost precincts of our being; so deep, indeed, that when we go there, we are no longer simply or exclusively our separate human selves but, by virtue of our own soul nature (for soul, as Plotinus tells us, is both partible among bodies and *indivisible*), our being verges too upon the Soul of the World. That same Soul of the World that—in giving concrete expression to the many seed-ideas or seminal sparks inherent within it—engenders those remarkable (and remarkably varied) forms we call creatures.

In origin and essence, these *animals* (note the root of the word) are of the very substance of the divine *anima mundi*—a fact which these creatures, like ourselves, naturally forget upon passage into a flesh and blood state of existence. And yet a residual awareness of the soul-essence that constitutes their common origin, that cosmic womb where they are not discrete self-interested organisms in noisome strife with one another but at one and at peace like the zodiac of stars encircling a single limitless sky . . . well, knowledge of that origin still sleeps, and will always sleep, in the creatures' heart of hearts. In the picture repainted by the poem, the song of Orpheus—tuned, like his lyre, to the music of the spheres and so spilling from that same sacred source—is reminding the animals of their divine origin. And it is that ineffably soothing recollection that is drawing them toward him while the influence of their purely biological and mutually hostile nature fades like a nightmare. As the poet sings, "Growl and roar, shriek and hiss/seemed small inside their hearts."

And we—we may perhaps intuitively perceive all this *if* we allow ourselves to imagine that animals, no less than humans, have a heart that is not merely a biomechanical pump; have, for instance, a Lion heart rather than a heart of Harvey. *If* we permit ourselves to understand, that is, that the wisdom forever inscribed in myth and fable is not mere poetic trope but deep spiritual and cosmological truth. Or rather, that these two (at least in the hands of a truly Orphic poet) are not two but one; that somewhere deep in the mind and soul there exists a place, a domain, a world where imaginative expression is known not as fictive but as revelatory of a deeper order of fact; not as illusion or attractive embellishment of some other order of truth but *archetypal verity.*

We can, if we wish, call this the imaginal realm. We can also call it the mythopoetic realm. Whatever we name it, it is the enchanted world opened for us by Orpheus's song, and our entrance into it is an effect of the archetypal presence of the lord of the realm who himself typifies the sacred origin and magical power of poetry and song. This is only logical: The imaginal, the mythopoetical, and the archetypal world opens to us, and so may be livingly experienced as a present reality (though of a different order than purely material reality) on account of the presence of the God by whose power and grace we may be—if our ears are open and our souls responsive to the possibility of participation—admitted as audience in this subtle amphitheater. This means, too—and again, this may be a kind of tautology—that it is our own soul's openness and attentiveness to the power of poetry that makes the God himself—Orpheus—*real* to us, and vice versa.

Does this mean "believing" in Orpheus in the way we usually understand this notion? The way we speak of "belief in God" as if the latter were radically other than we, an objective divine being whose existence and power do not essentially depend upon us, upon the human soul and its imaginative capacities? No. Rilke's Orpheus—and not only Rilke's—was never and can never be that sort of "God."

Instead, he appears and is real to us only in and through the agency of the poetic imagination which—in its very nature and act—*conjoins* the human and the divine, combines the creative activity of the individual *and* the world soul. In this respect, the poetic imagination is—inevitably—kin to the figure of Orpheus himself, who (like countless other legendary figures and demigods) is *neither* exclusively (transcendentally) divine *nor* purely human, but a kind of differential interface and intersection, which (if we were to name it) we might call the archetypal per se.

In fact, the act of imagination, in its metaphysical-cosmological-epistemological essence, is incompatible with "belief" in the usual sense—which term is sometimes employed as the translation of the mode of opinion Plato calls "*pistis*" in the parable of the Divided Line. For the category of "belief" always implies a critical difference in kind between the believer and what is believed in, making (as Plato's scheme implies) the existence of something ("God," for instance) a matter of *opinion*, a position manifestly open to disputation (of which, of course, there is no end).

Orpheus, on the other hand, may become real to us, not as some objective external figure but in and through the exercise of the faculty of creative (poetic and theophanic) imagination that is both the *gist* and *gift* of his archetypal being. In this respect, the figure of Orpheus may be understood to represent the soul's—our *psyche's*—own native poetic endowment, by means of which it may ultimately come to know the love and beauty for which it ever yearns not merely as objects of adoration or terror but as spiritual characteristics woven into the fabric of its own mature identity.

Two luminaries of myth and archetypal psychology may help shed further light on all this. Joseph Campbell, elucidating the kind of "creative mythology" that originates, in his view, in (where else?) ancient Greece, and which provides the historic point of departure for the spiritual activity we call art, writes of:

> . . . the Greek poets, artists, and philosophers for whom the gods (whether of the Homeric, the Orphic, or the Zoroastrian strains) were true as poetry is true. We may take it also to be the primitive (and proper) mythological point of view, as contrasted with the heavier positivistic; this latter is represented on the one hand by religious experiences of the literal sort, where the impact of a daemon, rising to the plane of consciousness from its place of birth on the level of the sentiments, is taken to be objectively real, and on the other, by science and political economy, for which only measurable facts are objectively real . . . . Whenever a myth has been taken literally its sense has been perverted; but also, reciprocally . . . whenever it has been dismissed as a mere priestly fraud or sign of inferior intelligence, truth has slipped out the other door.[123]

In *Revisioning Psychology,* James Hillman offers this related statement:

> The difference between religion and psychology lies not in our description of the Gods but in our action regarding them. Religion and psychology have care for the same ultimates, but religion approaches God with ritual, prayer, sacrifice, worship, creed. Gods are *believed* in and approached with religious methods. In archetypal psychology, Gods are *imagined.* They are approached through psychological methods of personifying, pathologizing, and psychologizing. They are formulated ambiguously, as metaphors for modes of experience and as numinous borderline persons. They are cosmic perspectives in which the soul participates. They are the lords of its realms of being, the patterns for its mimesis. The soul cannot be, except in one of their patterns.[124]

The two statements are very close. Hillman's, moreover, is central to the entire project of archetypal psychology and succinctly formulates insights essential to an understanding of the epistemological perspective that underlies the archetypal-psychological worldview.

The juxtaposition is particularly instructive, moreover, because, although Hillman here does not explicitly reference the "poetic basis of mind" so foundational for a psychology intent upon putting "soul at the center," Campbell does, and with a masterful concision that helps Hillman's archetypal view snap into focus. For Greek poets, artists, and philosophers, Campbell tells us, *"the gods . . . were true as poetry is true."*

Now this insight, which I take to be as integral to Hillman's vision as it is to Campbell's, has profound implications for archetypal psychology, implications we have already been attempting to elucidate. For it implies that the imaginal figure that grants us access to the archetypal intelligence of the Gods by rendering them available to the soul's imagination is none other than Orpheus himself. This means, in turn, that the mythic figure behind archetypal psychology itself, its presiding daemon or deific patron, if you will, is Orpheus.

Given Hillman's own continual emphasis on "the poetic basis of mind" and the aesthetic basis of his psychology, this should come as no surprise. In fact, Noel Cobb already provided lucid statement of this critical truth a quarter of a century ago. In his aptly named book *Archetypal Imagination: Glimpses of the Gods in Life and Art,* Cobb writes:

> Archetypal psychology, apart from its character as a polytheistic psychology and a theophanic psychology, is also an *aesthetic psychology*. And the mythic person within it must be an artist, even a poet. Now if we ask ourselves, what mythic figure is not only an artist, but an artist whose art is dedicated to the Gods, polytheistically, in their particularity, an artist who embodies the imagination and who is associated with the anima and the underworld and who sings of the beauty of Psyche, we must conclude that the mythic person for whom we have been searching is Orpheus.[125]

The comment that follows this citation in the *Soul History* is every bit as relevant here, in the context of this, the last and concluding lecture to this course:

> Given this archetypal perspective, it is logical that the founding tenets of Hillman's revisioning of his field find brilliantly imaginative expression in the poem cycle Rilke addresses to Orpheus, legendary well-spring of lyric poetry and archetypal psychology. So it is that the two streams we have been following all along reveal themselves united at the mythic source.[126]

Let us pause here, for just a moment, and review this result and its broader significance against the background of some of the themes that have occupied our attention throughout the course of these lectures.

The theme of the relation (or nonrelation) between the divine and the human has often concerned us and commanded center stage in our discussion of the *Elegies*. Yet, as I emphasize in both the *Soul History* and the introduction to my translation of the *Sonnets*, the *Sonnets* are a sensationally *different* work than are the *Elegies* and are so—from the first—quite tangibly and tellingly in just this critical regard. The *Elegies*, commencing with an all-too-human cry of despair, take the seemingly unbridgeable gap between divine and human consciousness as their agonized point of departure. The *Sonnets*, on the other hand, begin, with seemingly effortless ease, with—no manifestly human voice—but the image of a tree *and a God singing*—not to us, perhaps, and yet (as we've discussed) in a manner that invites our innermost soul into the presence of the God so that we may hear the music of his voice. Rather than abysmal gulf between the divine and the human being, we have something close to communion.

Even so, we should be aware that divine and human being are by no means *conflated* in the figure of Orpheus or the scene opened by his art. The third poem makes perfectly clear that the poet's own mortal consciousness remains persistently and keenly aware of the constitutive difference between these terms and in fact takes deliberation of this difference as its theme:

> A god is able. But how—tell me—do
> mortals follow through the narrow lye?
> Our sense is cleft. At the crossroads of two
> heartpaths, no temple bears Apollo's fire.
>
> Song, as you teach it, is not desire,
> not wooing something finally attained;
> Song is Being. The god's nature is gained,
> but when will we *be?*[127]

And so the difference—a difficult and in some wise painful one—remains. And yet, as we have seen, Orpheus is, from the first, far less distant and terrible than Rilke's angel. Accordingly, even this third poem, which appears early on in the cycle, suggests that the mortal poet may not only listen but—if he takes suitable measures—hope to sing truly; that is, *participate,* and actively so, in the archetypal being and essence of the God:

> This *is* not it youth—that you love—even if
> your voice poured paeans from your mouth. Sing

and forget that you sang out: it will end.
True singing demands a different breath.
A breath about nothing. A gust in the god. A wind.[128]

The model here is thus not—as seemed to be the case at the onset of the *Elegies*— one of unbridgeable ontological difference. For Orpheus is not, in fact, a *purely* transcendental divine being. While himself participating in divine cosmic intelligence, Orpheus, child of the Muse, effectively *reproduces* or images that divine harmony in the art of his song; *translates* purely invisible intelligible order into word and tone; into, that is, *aesthetic* form that is both sense perceptible, and so available to the human body, and culturally manifest, and so available to the mortal mind and imagination.

A liminal figure, Orpheus thus sings at the threshold between the divine and the human realms. His liminal, archetypal, imaginal domain represents the dynamic interface or intersection between, not only the polarities of the divine and the human, but between a host of related paired terms: eternity and time; heaven and earth; life and death; spirit and body. Rilke's sonnet cycle addresses all of these motifs, and more, quite explicitly and in multiple variations, and in each case the chief point is—not *elision* of the difference between the dualities that can (as we've repeatedly stressed) tear the soul in two and leave it hanging abysmally in between, but rather *differentiated and ultimately reunifying reconnection* in and through the middle term, the archetypal realm of soul entered by virtue of the thought of the heart, the creative act of the mythopoetic imagination, the personification of which is—Orpheus.

Still, the ability to listen and to hear Orpheus sing is one thing, but how do we manage to arrive on the scene in the first place? Of course, we can always pick up a book, but know all too well that, in fact, the end we are imagining here is not so easily attained. Rilke, after all, though a gifted and dedicated poet, did not arrive at this Orpheus—a far deeper and more meaningful figure than the one in his "Orpheus, Eurydice, Hermes"—until he was nearing the end of his life. Have we any right to expect much quicker progress?

We may arrive at Orpheus—and that means we may find ourselves in the imaginal archetypal world opened by and through him, recognizing it as our soul's own world, the native realm where we are most at home—by (naturally) walking the path of soul. This means something like following John Keats's recipe and bringing Mind, Heart, and the trouble, joy, and sorrow of the World effectively to bear upon one another as we make and remake our selves as soul; something like following in Psyche's footsteps as she finds herself cast out of the everyday world to become the bride of Eros, loves and loses him and, devastated and all but physically dead, embarks upon the long travail of her labors; something like living the archetypal phases of the soul depicted, with such delicate symbolic genius, in the sequence of the Lady and the Unicorn tapestries, living, loving, dying, and practicing our scales so that we come, at least and at last, to that *fifth* stage of contemplative wisdom, when we are inwardly clear enough to catch the image of the spirit-self—the magical unicorn—in the mirror of our own souls. For all these paths, as well as the winding trail of Rilke's poetic journey, are, in archetypal essence, one road. And always, inevitably, wherever and whoever we are, it is the road that lies beyond the threshold of our too familiar experience, the road less traveled by.

Yet never mind the *finish* of such work; how do we even step forward and make a start? Recall that very first scene painted in Rilke's *Sonnets*, the magic circle gathering around the figure of Orpheus, singing. In addressing that scene, we spoke of sinking into our innermost being so that we might begin to listen in, like the animals. In this connection, we may ask: What, or who, is it in us that grants such imaginative permission, empowers the thought of our heart, and so allows us, too, to remember our own human soul's original participation in *anima mundi,* the soul of the world?

We naturally gain access to the soul in the world through the soul in us; enter the realm of *anima mundi* by way of *anima.* And so, after the first and before the third poem in the sequence, the second:

> And it was almost a girl who emerged from
> the consonant pleasure of song and lyre
> and shone clear through her shady spring attire
> and made her bed within my ear's deep drum.
>
> And slept in me, And her sleep was everything.
> The trees I always marveled at, those
> palpable distances, the deeply felt meadows
> and every wonder that touched my human being.
>
> She slept the world.[129]

"Almost" meaning: no actual, no real girl, of course, but a daimonic or archetypal presence and power like that possessed by a real girl . . . like Vera, that beautiful young dancer. Or rather, the other way around: the daimonic power of that imaginal Eurydice figure, that archetypal Kore, that a "real" girl, like Vera, may participate in and in so doing be—both herself (even, and indeed especially, in her dying) and more than that; be, for instance, an embodiment of soul and inspiration for a poet's song.

Let us recall Rilke's imaginative recollection of Vera, and the thought of her heart, gathered from the lines of the diary lent to him by Vera's mother. Rilke articulates "the two outermost boundaries of her [Vera's] *pure intuition"*:

> . . . *this,* that suffering is an error, a dull misapprehension arising from the physical that drives its wedge, its stony wedge, into the unity between heaven and earth; and, at the other extreme, the oneness of her wide-open heart with the existing and enduring world, this assent to life, this joyous impassioned communing to the very last moment with her native earth—ah, with only the earth? Nay (and this she could not know in these first attacks of breakup and parting)—with the Whole, with much more than the earth. Oh, how, how she loved, how she reached out with the antennae of her heart beyond all that can be grasped or encompassed here.[130]

That first "outermost boundary," touching on the extreme of purely physical exigencies, should not, of course, be taken as a general dismissal of the role of suffering (Keats's "world of trouble and sorrow") in soul-making.

Rilke, of all poets, would never sanction any such. Anyone who has ever had anything to do with a case of terminal illness in a young, spiritually vibrant person knows the tragic contours of the special situation to which Rilke refers here. The second "outermost boundary"—the one touching the purely spiritual dimension of Vera's being and imminent nonbeing—can help us understand another dimension of that place that qualifies as the origin and end of the poem, that (nonphysical) heart-space which the poem evokes and, from start to finish, inhabits; that "clear freed forest" where the souls of animals gather to listen to Orphic song.

So then, two additional amplifications.

First, the place—this imaginal place—is, as Rilke indicates in his letter, both fully immanent—wholly of the Earth—and more than that; beyond any mode of thought that sees the Earth itself and all matter of things of the Earth as somehow essentially discontinuous with the entire Cosmos; with the light of the Sun, Moon, and Stars; the movement of the Planets and Seasons and all divine rhythms that form the beating heart of the Cosmos, and—even beyond the spiritual Life of the whole Cosmos itself—the divine universal mind of which the Cosmos itself is an image and emanation. This means that the Orphic voice speaking through the poet Rilke can, and consistently does, connect the most sensuously precise, the most fully embodied experience of visible things *here* (an orange, a fountain, a white horse; a child and the ball she throws into the air; a dancer) with the vast, the illimitable reaches of spiritual mind and heart-space:

> Dancer: transposition
> of transience into the flow of your form: how you offered it there!
> And the swirl at the end; this tree made of motion,
> did it not fully capture the far-flung year?
>
> Did not—so your just finished swinging would whirl round it—the crown
> suddenly bloom with stillness? And over, above,
> wasn't it sun, wasn't it summer, up there pouring down
> the immeasurable warmth of your love?[131]

Second, the Tree itself. This is, of course, no ordinary tree. As I explain in the introduction to my translation of the *Sonnets*, it is the Rilkean representation of the World Tree, the sacred place that—connecting above and below—qualifies as the symbolic center of the universe, and from which point the universe itself (like the world of the *Sonnets*) grows. Campbell also calls this the "World Navel," the spiritual origin and end of the universe, which is, significantly enough, also the alpha and omega of the hero-journey and so the key to all spiritual renewal:

> For the hero as the incarnation of God is himself the navel of the world, the umbilical point through which the energies of eternity break into time. Thus the World Navel is the symbol of the continuous creation: the mystery of the maintenance of the world through that continuous miracle of vivification which wells within all things.[132]

The Rilkean image of the Tree and the divine singer associated with it stands as the Orphic equivalent of this motif, which appears elsewhere, as Campbell tells us, in the form of *the biblical Tree of Life*, the *Boddhi tree under which the Buddha achieved enlightenment,* and the *Holy Rood* upon which the God-Man was crucified.

Judaism, Buddhism, Christianity all possess their archetypal world-tree. Yet, for all the worth of these well-established world religions, they fall under the aegis of—and here I employ the categories of Campbell's *Masks of God*—either Eastern (Buddhist) or Occidental (Jewish and Christian) mythology. None of these images, that is, emerges from the singular character of that other major mythological kind Campbell christens *Creative Mythology*, and which he understands to have devolved—not from sacerdotal or priestly religions—but from the ancient Greek poets, artists, and philosophers. Both Bruno Snell's and James Hillman's work eloquently attest to the truth that this mythological heritage may—indeed must—be considered intrinsically poetic and soul-centered; at once and inseparably archetypally psychological and aesthetic. It is a lineage that flows from the deep heart's core; a tradition that reserves ultimate value for—no creed of belief, no religious doctrine or code of moral law, no set of sacred rites or spiritual practices—but the inexhaustible spring of the Creative Imagination that wells forth from *anima mundi*, and the Orpheus in each of us that listens and sings in concert with the Soul of the World in the style unique to the mature identity of the individual soul.

And the herald of the new beginning ("neuer Anfang") that may dawn by virtue of this vision *(The New—Master, do you hear /it rumbling and drumming? / Harbingers appear /and herald its coming*[133]*)*, forerunner of the modern renaissance of this classical tradition?

Let us listen to the voice that speaks quietly—quietly, and yet as strongly and surely as the sound of spring spreading over the face of the earth.

Already—listen—you can hear the first song
of the harrows; again the human drumming
in the self-contained stillness of the strong
early spring earth. That which is coming

seems somehow unspoiled. What's come to you
so often already, comes once more
as if it were new. Always hoped for
you never seized it. It seized you.

Even the oak leaves that hung on through the snow
appear, in the evening, a future brown.
Sometimes, breezes let one another know.

The bushes are black. Yet the piles of dung
that lie in the fields are a still darker tone.
And every hour that passes, grows still more young.[134]

Notes

Preface

[1] Daniel Joseph Polikoff, *In the Image of Orpheus: Rilke—A Soul History* (Wilmette, IL: Chiron Publications, 2011).
[2] Why are these lectures appearing in print first now, eight years after their composition? The pandemic years brought a hiatus in my focus on Rilke in favor of other (Emerson-related) work that culminated in two Covid-related titles (*Reset or Renaissance: An American Scholar's Covid Chronicle,* and *Apocalypse of the Modern Mind: Covid and the Dialectic of Enlightenment* (Spencertown NY: PortalBooks, 2024 and 2025 respectively). This year, on the other hand, I have turned significant attention back to Rilke in preparation for the International Rilke Society's gathering honoring the poet's 150th birthday in the city of his birth (Prague). Internally as well as externally, it finally seems high time to make these lectures available to a wider public.
[3] The author will elaborate the idea of the Sophianic Cross in future writings.

First Lecture

[4] Rainer Maria Rilke, "Eingang" in *Buch der Bilder* (*The Book of Images*). Translation by Daniel Joseph Polikoff (DJP).
[5] James Hillman, *Revisioning Psychology* (NY: HarperCollins, 1975).
[6] James Hillman, *The Thought of the HEART* and *the SOUL of the World* (Dallas, Spring Publications, 1993). The volume contains Hillman's reworkings of two separate lectures. *The Thought of the* Heart material was first given as a lecture at the Eranos Conference

in Ascona Switzerland in 1979. *Anima Mundi: The Return of the Soul to the World* (which figures centrally in the fifth Rilke lecture here) was first published in 1982 in *Spring* as a slightly revised version of a lecture given (in Italian translation) in Florence, Italy.

[7] James Hillman, *The Myth of Analysis* (NY: HarperCollins, 1978).

[8] James Hillman, *The Dream and the Underworld* (NY: Harper-Colllins, 1979).

[9] Hillman, *The Thought of the Heart*, 39.

[10] Ibid., 40.

[11] Ibid., 40-41.

[12] C. G. Jung, *Memories, Dreams, and Reflections* (NY: Vintage Books, 1965), 185-186.

[13] Friedrich Schiller, *On the Aesthetic Education of Man in a Series of Letters*, translated by Elizabeth M. Wilkinson and L.A. Willoughby (Oxford: Oxford UP, 1982).

[14] C. G. Jung, *Archetypes of the Collective Unconscious*, *CW* 9, i: ¶ 59 (Princeton UP, 1969).

[15] René Descartes, *Discourse on Method* (Indiana, The Liberal Arts Inc., 1950).

[16] Richard Tarnas, *The Passion of the Western Mind* (NY: Harmony Books, 1991).

[17] James Joyce, *Portrait of the Artist as a Young Man* (NY: Bantam Books, 1992).

[18] C. G. Jung, *The Red Book* (NY: W.W. Norton, 2009).

[19] R.M. Rilke, "Der Panther" in *Neue Gedichte* (*New Poems*). translated by DJP.

[20] Daniel Joseph Polikoff, *In the Image of Orpheus: Rilke—A Soul History* (Wilmette, IL: Chiron Publications, 2011).

[21] Daniel Joseph Polikoff, *Rue Rilke* (Asheville, NC: Chiron Publications, 2016). In light of the enormous attention devoted to issues of race in recent times, it may be noted here that *Rue Rilke*, the text of which was written in 1993, binds together the author's search for the roots of Rilke's poetic vision and antideath-penalty activism focused on the effort to stave off an impending execution of a Black man in Texas. As such, it offers a soul-spiritual attempt to deal with the legacy of racial prejudice in a manner markedly different from the more ideologically-oriented treatments of the matter (such as "critical race theory") current today, and so offers an alternative avenue of approach sourced in archetypal psychological and poetic insight; in, that is, "the thought of the heart."

Second Lecture

[22] James Hillman, "Peaks and Vales" in *Puer Papers* (Dallas, TX: Spring Publications, 1989), 54.
[23] Charles Wright, "Indian Summer II," as cited in Polikoff, *In the Image of Orpheus*, 684.
[24] James Hollis, *The Archetypal Imagination* (College Station TX, Texas A&M UP, 2000), 14.
[25] See Plato's famous discussion of the Divided Line and parable of the cave in Book 6 of *The Republic.*
[26] See the fourth lecture for reference to and discussion of aspects of Romanyshyn's work.
[27] Bruno Snell, *The Discovery of the Mind* (Tacoma, WA: Angelico Press, 2013), 19.
[28] Ibid., 8.
[29] Ibid., ix.
[30] Ibid., 17.
[31] Ibid.
[32] Ibid., 60.
[33] Ibid., 44.
[34] Ibid., 45.
[35] Sappho, tr. by Mary Barnard as poem #47 in *Sappho* (Boston, Shambala Publications, 1958), 65.
[36] Snell, *Discovery,* 60.
[37] Ibid., 61.
[38] In his early twenties, Rilke wrote a series of eleven substantial poems (all of which display pronounced dramatic and narrative as well as lyrical elements) expressing his own (quite critical) view of the figure of Jesus. The work, which he titled *Christus: Elf Visionen* (*Christ: Twelve Visions*) played a crucial role in Rilke's psychological, spiritual and poetic development. For a relatively detailed discussion of this work, including the historical and critical background of its composition, see the second chapter of Polikoff, *In the Image of Orpheus,* pp. 27-59. The bilingual source is Rainer Maria Rilke, *Visions of Christ*, edited by Siegfried Mandel, translated by Aaron Kramer (Boulder, CO: University of Colorado Press, 1967).
[39] For English translations of these two important (and little known) early works see, Rainer Maria Rilke, *Larenopfer (Offering to the Lares),* translated by Alfred de Zayas (LA: Red Hen Press, 2005) and

Rainer Maria Rilke, *Traumgekrönt* (*Dream-Crowned*), translated by Lorne Mook (New Orleans, University of New Orleans Press, 2010). The first chapter of *In the Image of Orpheus* contains my own translations of several poems from these collections.

[40] Rilke's poem "From the Lookout" (from *Larenopfer*) as translated in Polikoff, *In the Image of Orpheus*, 16.

[41] Rilke's poem (XV in *Traumgekrönt*) as translated in Polikoff, *In the Image of Orpheus*, 23.

Third Lecture

[42] Rainer Maria Rilke, first poem in *Das Buch vom mönchischen Leben (The Book of Monastic Life),* first volume of *Das Stundenbuch (The Book of Hours),* Tr. by DJP.

[43] Hollis, *Archetypal Imagination*, 14.

[44] The word "scientist" was not coined until the 19th century, and "science," as we think of it today, did not exist before the Enlightenment era or even 19th century. Study of the cosmos and of natural phenomena generally proceeded under the aegis of "natural history" or "natural philosophy."

[45] Developments associated with Luther and Galileo did not inaugurate this split but rather confirmed and hardened a division already prepared by prior intellectual historical trends, including those associated with scholasticism and the nominalism of William of Ockham. For a more detailed discussion, see Polikoff, *Apocalypse of the Modern Mind* (Spencertown NY: Portalbooks, 2025), Ch. 6, especially 156-58. See also the discussion of the doctrine of "pure nature" ("Natura Pura") in Michael Martin, *The Submerged Reality: Sophiology and the Turn to a Poetic Metaphysics* (Kettering, OH: Angelico Press, 2015), Ch. 1.

[46] Richard Dawkins, *The God Delusion* (NY: Mariner Books, 2008).

[47] See Polikoff, *In the Image of Orpheus*, Ch. 3.

[48] Lou Andreas-Salome, "Vom religiösen Affekt" and "Der Realismus in der Religion" in Lou Andreas-Salome, *Aufsätze und Essays,* Band 1: Religion (Taching am See: MedienEditionWelsch, 2011), 49-59, 59-91. Unfortunately, Lou Andreas-Salome's essays on psychology and religion are not available in English.

[49] Ibid.

[50] See, for instance, the first chapter ("Personifying or Imagining Things)" of *Revisioning Psychology.*

[51] This, of course, is a quintessentially Romantic theme, but I here cite sources that exercised tangible influence that can directly be read from Rilke's biography (Rilke did read Emerson, in translation). I do not think Romantic poets and philosophers were the most critical influences for Rilke in the formative stage of his development, unless one defines Emerson (or even Nietzsche) as essentially Romantic. The German Romantic poet Friedrich Hölderlin (1770-1843) emerged as a hugely important influence for Rilke (as did, to some degree, Goethe (11749-1832): formally speaking, these are the two greatest influences on Rilke's *Elegies*) but did not play that role in his early, formative period.
[52] See Andreas-Salome's "Der Realismus in der Religion" (in *Aufsätze und Essays, Band 1*), 59-91.
[53] Rainer Maria Rilke, *Rilke's Book of Hours,* translated by Anita Barrows and Joanna Macy (NY: Riverhead Books, 1996), 74.
[54] Rilke, "Ich finde dich in all diese Dingen" (*Book of Monastic Life,* poem #22), translated by DJP.
[55] *Rilke's Book of Hours,* translated by Barrows and Macy, 81.
[56] Ibid.
[57] Rilke, "Du bist der Tiefste" *Book of Monastic Life,* poem #46, translated by DJP.
[58] Rilke translated by DJP.
[59] Ernest Fenellosa and Ezra Pound, *The Chinese Written Character as a Medium for Poetry* (NY: Fordham UP, 2011).
[60] Kathleen Raine, "The Use of the Beautiful" in *Defending Ancient Springs* (Stockbridge, Mass: Lindisfarne Press, 1985), 174.
[61] Ibid., 172.
[62] Ibid., 175.

Fourth Lecture

[63] Polikoff, *In the Image of Orpheus*, 207.
[64] Rainer Maria Rilke, *Diaries of a Young Poet,* translated by Edward Snow and Michael Winkler (NY: W.W. Norton, 1998), 220
[65] Ibid., 175-176.
[66] Ibid., 162-163.
[67] For a detailed elaboration of the maiden, or Kore archetype, see Safron Rossi, *The Kore Goddess: A Mythology and Psychology* (Arroyo Grande, CA: Winter Press, 2021). The centrality of the Kore in Rilke's psychology indicates that (as one might expect), the

Kore may function as a symbol of the self as soul for men as well as women.

[68] Ibid., 156.

[69] Robert D. Romanyshyn, "Yes, Indeed! Do Call the World the Vale of Soul Making" in *Ways of the Heart: Essays Towards an Imaginal Psychology* (Pittsburgh, PA: Trivium Publications, 2002), 65.

[70] Gaston Bachelard, *The Poetics of Reverie* (Boston, MA: Beacon Press, 1971).

[71] Monika Wikman, *Pregnant Darkness: Alchemy and the Rebirth of Consciousness* (Berwick, MN: Nicholas-Hays, 2004), xix.

[72] Rainer Maria Rilke, fragment in *In und Nach Worpswede,* (Frankfurt am Main: Insel Verlag, 2000), 17.

[73] Polikoff, *In the Image of Orpheus*, 202:

> To live half-unconscious, and half in haste,
> to set down what one saw—how, and where;
> to act with purpose, and then once more to wander
> in the unknown, alone, and free of care—:
> here these lovely girls fit this mold;
> half held in thrall, yet already seizing hold . . .

See also Snow, *Diaries of a Young Poet*, 175, where these lines appear in Edward Snow's translation.

[74] The phrase appears in Rilke's poem, "Von den Mädchen I (Girls I) in his *Das Buch der Bilder* (*The Book of Images)* as translated by DJP.

Fifth Lecture

[75] James Hillman, *The Thought of the HEART* and *the SOUL of the World* (Dallas, Spring Publications, 1993).

[76] Ibid., 69-70.

[77] Harold Bloom, *The Visionary Company: A Reading of English Romantic Poetry* (Ithaca, NY: Cornell UP, 1971).

[78] William Wordsworth, *The Excursion*, Prospectus, l. 24, in English Romantic Writers, ed. David Perkins (NY: Harcourt Brace, 1967), 301.

[79] Walt Whitman, "Song of Myself" in *Leaves of Grass* (NY: The New American Library Inc., 1980), 49.

[80] Hillman, *Soul of the World,* 101.

[81] Ibid., 109.

[82] Ibid.
[83] Big cats, whose movement is characterized by fluid rhythmic motion, may also fittingly be associated with the heart and so passionate nature in contrast to two other major classes of mammals: the rodents, which are primarily nerve-sense (and so "heady") organisms, and ungulates, which may be associated with the (unconscious will forces of the) metabolic system.
[84] R.M. Rilke, "Der Panther" in *Neue Gedichte* (*New Poems*) translated by DJP.
[85] "Früher Apollo" ("Early Apollo"). The next poem described is "Römische Fontäne" ("Roman Fountain"). For an English translation of Rilke's *Neue Gedichte* see *New Poems,* Rainer Maria Rilke, translated and edited by Edward Snow (Berkeley, CA: North Point Press, 1984).
[86] See the next (sixth) lecture.
[87] Paul Brunton (1898 – 1981), author of numerous books on spiritual subjects, was instrumental in bringing Eastern spiritual wisdom and meditative practices to the West. See, for instance, Paul Brunton, *The Wisdom of the Overself* (Berkeley, CA: North Atlantic Books, 2015).
[88] Here the reference is to the Navajo culture's idea of Walking in Beauty, which is purportedly no mere concept but understood as a path of life.
[89] Rainer Maria Rilke, *Duino Elegies,* translated by J.B. Leishman and Stephen Spender (NY: W.W. Norton, 1939), First Elegy, ll. 4-7.
[90] C.S. Lewis, *Till We Have Faces* (NY: HarperOne, 2017).
[91] Hillman, *Soul of the World,* 109.

Sixth Lecture

[92] James Hillman, *The Soul's Code: In Search of Character and Calling* (NY: Random House, 1996).
[93] James Hillman, *The Force of Character and the Lasting Life* (NY: Random House, 1999).
[94] John Keats, Letter to George and Georgiana Keats, April 21, 1819. *Selected Poems and Letters by John Keats,* Ed. Douglas Bush (Boston: Houghton-Mifflin, 1959), 288.
[95] Ibid.
[96] Ibid., 288-89.

[97] C.G. Jung, *On the Nature of the Psyche,* (Princeton, NJ: Princeton UP, 1960), 100.

[98] We touch here on rather treacherous metaphysical ground, the investigation of which would take us beyond the province of these lectures. Nonetheless, Jung himself does not shy away from associating "the sparks of the soul" with the Platonic forms that, philosophically considered, constitute the ground of "the archetypes." In the *Nature of the Psyche,* Jung, glossing Khunrath and the Wisdom of Solomon, writes that in the primordial chaos "there are to be found the 'fiery sparks of the soul of the world [anima mundi] as pure Formae Rerum essentiales." These *formae* correspond to the Platonic Ideas, from which one could equate the scintillae with the archetypes on the assumption that the Forms "stored up in a supracelestial place" are a "philosophical version of the latter." Jung, Nature of the Psyche, 101.

[99] Ralph Waldo Emerson, "Self-Reliance" in *Emerson: Essays and Lectures* (NY: Library of America/Literary Classics of the United States, 1983), 257.

[100] Rainer Maria Rilke, *The Notebooks of Malte Laurids Brigge,* translated by M.D. Herter Norton ((NY: W.W. Norton, 1949), 14-15.

[101] Ibid., 13.

[102] The reference is to the Musée de Cluny in Paris, where the sequence of six famous late medieval/early Renaissance tapestries are housed. This is one of two well-preserved unicorn-themed tapestry sequences. The other, *very different* sequence, hangs in the Cloisters in the Metropolitan Museum of Art in New York.

[103] Gottfried Büttner, *The Lady and the Unicorn: The Development of the Human Soul as Pictured in the Cluny Tapestries,* translated by Roland Everett (Stroud, England: Hawthorn Press, 1995).

[104] C. G. Jung, *Psychology and Alchemy* (Princeton, NJ: Princeton UP, 1968), 436.

[105] Ibid., 437.

[106] Ibid., 438.

[107] James Hillman, *The Myth of Analysis* (Evanston, IL: Northwestern University Press, 1972), 169ff.

[108] James Hillman, *Healing Fiction* (Woodstock, CT: Spring Publication, 1983).

[109] Rilke to Lou Andreas-Salomé, Jan. 20, 1912 in *Letters of Rainer Maria Rilke,* 1910-1926, translated by Jane Bannard Greene and M.D. Herter Norton (NY: W.W. Norton: 1947/72), 45.

Seventh Lecture

[110] Rainer Maria Rilke, *Duino Elegies,* translated by J.B. Leishman and Stephen Spender (NY: W.W. Norton, 1939), First Elegy, ll. 1-5.
[111] *The Holy Bible*, King James Version, Psalm 130.
[112] Rainer Maria Rilke, *Sonnets to Orpheus,* introduced and edited by Daniel Joseph Polikoff (Kettering, OH: Angelico Press, 2015), 6-7.
[113] Rilke, sixth poem in *The Book of Monastic Life,* translated by DJP.
[114] Rilke, First Elegy, Leishman and Spender translation, ll. 57-58.
[115] Rilke, letter to Witold von Hulewicz, November 13, 1925 in *Letters* (tr. by Greene and Herter-Norton), 372.
[116] Keats, *Selected Poems and Letters,* 288.
[117] *The Holy Bible*, King James Version, Psalm 130.
[118] Hollis, *Archetypal Imagination*, 14.
[119] The reference is to the classic work by Joseph Campbell, *The Hero with a Thousand Faces.*
[120] Paul Brunton, *Essays on the Quest* (York Beach, MN: Samuel Weiser, Inc., 1984), Ch. 5.
[121] The term "Weltinnenraum" appears in an untitled, uncollected poem by Rilke (written in his journal in 1914) that begins "Es winkt zu Fühlung fast aus allen Dingen." Rainer Maria Rilke, *Die Gedichte* (Frankfurt am Main: Insel Verlag, 1995), 878. The poem with an English translation by David Young may be found in the Corland Review at https://archive.cortlandreview.org/features/13/summer/young.php. The idea of "world-inner-space" is not, however, peculiar to this poem, but informs much of Rilke's later work. Although the phrase itself does not appear in the Elegies, the idea underlies the implicit metaphysics of the poem and indeed Rilke's poetic worldview generally.

Eighth Lecture

[122] All translations in this lecture are from Rainer Maria Rilke, *Sonnets to Orpheus,* translated by Daniel Jospeh Polikoff (Kettering, OH: Angelico Press, 2015). The Sonnets—hereafter abbreviated as SO—are in two parts. This first sonnet of the first part is therefore identified as I, 1. Subsequent citations follow the same format.

[123] Joseph Campbell, *The Mythic Dimension, Selected Essays 1959-1987*, Ed. Antony Van Couvering (San Francisco, HarperCollins, 1997), 27.
[124] Hillman, *Revisioning Psychology,* 169.
[125] Noel Cobb, *Archetypal Imagination: Glimpses of the Gods in Life and Art* (Hudson, NY: Lindisfarne Press, 1992), 236.
[126] Polikoff, *In the Image of Orpheus,* 628.
[127] SO I, 3.
[128] Ibid.
[129] SO I, 2.
[130] Letter to Gertrude Ouckama Knoop, January 1922. *Letters of Rainer Maria Rilke 1910-1926*, translated by Jane Bannard Greene and M.D. Herter Norton (New York, London: W. W. Norton, 1947, 1972), 284.
[131] SO II, 18.
[132] Joseph Campbell, *The Hero with a Thousand Faces* (New York: MJF Books, 1949), 41.
[133] SO I, 18.
[134] SO II, 25.

www.ingramcontent.com/pod-product-compliance
Lightning Source LLC
LaVergne TN
LVHW090403210926
848480LV00002B/430
9781685036751